PRAISE FOR

Empowering the Children

★

A few days after I began reading Karen Szillat's *Empowering the Children,* *including the section on* "guns and kids: stopping our future dead in their tracks!" twenty children and six adults were shot to death in a school in Sandy Hook Connecticut. Karen Szillat would not have imagined nor wished for more powerful evidence that her book, her philosophy and her vision for empowering children and the educators who love them is needed now.

Szillat focuses on twelve universal values, indeed what I regard to be *fundamental values*...Using each of these fundamental ideas as a chapter theme, Karen draws on her rich experience to articulate strategies and describe do-able learning activities that are easily integrated into daily practice. These are the kind of learnings that must underlie all of our educational efforts; this is not just another "subject" in school; this is foundation upon which we teach. I am happy to recommended this book to anyone who genuinely cares about kids and their future.

— **John McDonnell Tierney, Ph.D., Executive Director,**
The Peaceful Educator Foundation

Courage is not the absence of fear, but rather the judgment that some-thing else is more important than fear." I thought only I went around quoting that. Turns out this book is FULL of ideas I not only love and endorse, but ideas I can use anytime I'm dealing with people—from tots to tyrants. If you like insight (and punchlines! Tons of punchlines!), pick it up!

— **Lenore Skenazy, Author of the book and blog** *Free-Range Kids*

If you are a parent or educator of young children, this book is a must-read! Filled with heartwarming anecdotes and helpful activities, Karen Szillat expertly teaches us how to empower children as young as three years old to become successful, caring, contributing members of society. A truly remarkable book!

> – Diane Ross-Glazer, Ph.D., Author of *Parenting as a Second Language: Using the Power of the Head-Heart Connection to Speak Your Child's Language*

This book combines personal and professional experience with young children to create a warmhearted and practical guide. Parents and teachers will find it engaging and useful.

> – Dr. Shirin Sherkat, Parent Strategist and Author of *Create Happy Kids*

Karen knows what it means to be in community. As a single mom trying to raise responsible children, I am so impressed with the many ways Karen shows us to get kids to feel like part of a community. When kids have the opportunity to give and share what they have, it changes them for life. Get a pen and paper out because you will want to take notes when reading Karen's book *Empowering the Children*.

> – Laurie Ann Hardie, Author of *Did Not See That Coming*, KOMO Newsradio Total Traffic Network

Karen Szillat is destined to become known as the Pied Piper of "Pre-schooldom." In this book, she speaks with a voice that demonstrates both a deep understanding of the pre-school mind and each child's unlimited potential. The same unique perspective, the same joy and love that infused her classroom, has now at last burst onto the scene in the form of a book that will shock and delight the reader with unforgettable and often humorous ways to incorporate morality and right action into the everyday lessons we seek to teach this new generation of souls.

> – Marianne Stanley, Human Services Attorney and former family teacher for Father Flanagan's Boys Town

Karen Szillat's *Empowering the Children* is a refreshing book that honors children as whole people, deserving our love and respect. *Empowering the Children* gives parents a wise approach to parenting that often is not heard. As a parent of two daughters, I have worked to empower them and give them the tools to be strong, self-assured young women. Karen's book gives me a great perspective for additional ways to do this and keep them safe at the same time.

– Donna Price, Author of *Launching Your Dreams* and *Coaching Staff for Success*

Parents are the experts on their own children. Effective teachers honor this and team with parents to help children thrive beyond the walls of the home and the classroom. *Empowering the Children* describes strategies for developing children who become positive world citizens.

– Dauna Easley, Author of *TEACH...To Change Lives*

Just what the doctor ordered! This book is brilliantly written, so very engaging, and a fantastic read. Every parent, teacher, and child-care provider on the planet must read this if they are to join Karen Szillat in her vision of raising a generation of peace loving children to become conscious citizens of the world and the leaders of tomorrow. Bravo! This work is a masterpiece!

– Patrick Snow, International Best-Selling Author of *Creating Your Own Destiny* and *The Affluent Entrepreneur*

Empowering the Children offers a straightforward prescription for communication techniques that can change the way parents speak with, and listen to, their children. It's a "must-read" book that offers powerful ways to build and strengthen relationships.

– Susan Friedmann, International Best-Selling Author of *Riches in Niches: How to Make it BIG in a Small Market*

Don't buy *Empowering the Children* unless you want your children to have a great value system, be tremendous problem solvers, and have the confidence to try new things. Karen has hit another homerun; I only wish this book was available when my children were little. Buy it, read it, live it.

– Andy Fracica, MBA, Author of *Navigating the Marketing Maze*

Karen's wit, charm, and undeniable gift for connecting to the young is displayed beautifully within these pages. Her words offer insight to anyone who has the gift of being around God's innocence—the children.

– Rowena Portch, Author of the *Spirian Saga*

Karen's passion and respect for children shine through the pages of this book.

– Judy Hoff, Author of *Healing the Hole in Your Heart: True Stories of Hope and Restoration*

If you are interested in establishing a fun and flexible environment where the children have the opportunity to explore, interact with other children, play and learn at their own level, this is the book for you. If you are interested in helping kids grow into the adults we need tomorrow, this is the book for you.

– H.C. (Joe) Raymond, Author of *Embracing Change From the Inside Out*

Karen practices a child-centered, developmentally appropriate curriculum that focuses on building strong citizens.

– Bruce Raine, Author of *Attitude Determines Destiny*

You'll never look at your children in the same way again after reading this book! You will see more wisdom, generosity, love of all people and the world than you ever imagined.

– June Kerr, Author of *Rabboni, My Love: A Memoir of Jesus' Wife, Mary Magdalene*

By reminding us of what is truly important, Karen helps adults focus on making a huge difference for their children today. Our kids are ready!

— **Randall Broad, Author of**
It's an Extraordinary Life: Don't Miss It

If you want your children to live in a world that is better than the one we live in today, pick up this book! Life lessons that will last a lifetime can begin now.

— **Gigi Murfitt, Parent of two amazing sons and Author of**
Caregivers' Devotions to GO **and** *My Message is C.L.E.A.R.*

Optimistic, inspiring, and a memorable read. This book should be required reading for everyone who works with young children!

— **Gabe Murfitt, Author of** *My Message is C.L.E.A.R.*

Easy to read and practical for kids of all ages. The world would be a better place if we all picked one strategy from this book.

— **Kate Phillips, Author of** *The Financial Stress Solution*

I wish this book had been available when my kids were young. I will gift it to new generations of parents.

— **Joy Evans Peterson, M.A. Author of**
Discovering a Dynamic Marriage

Empowering the Children is a truly insightful book that reveals how children can make a difference in the world.

— **Theresa Callahan, Author of** *Managing for Performance:*
Building Accountability for Team Success

This book brings practical solutions and fun ideas for parents and teachers to better support kids on their quest to become global citizens.

— **Joanna Cummings, Author of** *Kick Butts Take Names*

Karen Szillat shows how a combination of clear boundaries and enjoyment always have a place in an enriching classroom and home environment.

– Sherri Nickols, Author of *Sexy and Sparkling After 40*

Alligators, firefighters, science, the Tooth Fairy....What more do you want out of a book?!

– Katie Munoz, Co-Author of *Get Organized Today*

Empowering the Children shows how parents and educators can guide children through the difficult journeys of life and answer the questions that we all wish children didn't have to face.

– Janette Turner, Author of *Penning Your Memoir*

Empowering the
CHILDREN

12 Universal Values Your Child Must
Learn to Succeed in Life

★

Karen Szillat

AVIVA
PUBLISHING
NEW YORK

Published by:
Aviva Publishing
Lake Placid, NY
518-523-1320
www.avivapubs.com

Please address all inquiries to:

Karen Szillat
Karen@KarenSzillat.com
www.EmpoweringTheChildren.com

ISBN: 978-1-938686-29-0

Library of Congress Control Number: 2013900161

Editor: Tyler Tichelaar

Cover and Interior Book Design: Fusion Creative Works,
www.fusioncw.com

First Edition

For additional copies please visit:
www.EmpoweringTheChildren.com

Author's Note

★

Although this book is a manual for parents and teachers of young children from approximately two to eight years of age, it includes a variety of stories from my life to help illustrate important principles and to demonstrate how I learned to be a better parent and teacher through trial and error. There are many stories I could have included but did not, due to lack of space. Some stories have been simplified for clarity of reading, and some names have been changed or excluded for privacy. All attempts have been made to be factual; any errors are unintentional and based solely on my memories.

Dedication

★

To my husband John: You have always been my greatest supporter and have been encouraging me to write for fifteen years. *Du bist mein Schatz. Vielen Dank!*

To my daughter Michaele: I am so very proud of you. I hope this book helps you feel empowered today and tomorrow.

To Jessica, my preschool partner and friend: Thank you for inspiring me to create new ways of teaching things with our kids and for making me love coming to work every day.

To Sasha Ernst Torkildson: Without your sweet smiling face, I might never have found my calling. Thanks for empowering your high school babysitter!

To all of the children, families, and early educators I've had the pleasure of working with over the years: Thank you for sharing your experiences, talents, and dreams with me. I am forever grateful. This book is for you.

Acknowledgments

★

Nothing is created in a vacuum, including this book. I have learned from many people in order to put these words on paper. Some of these lessons were learned as I was growing up and some more recently as an adult, but the importance of the lessons had no bearing on the age of the person at the time.

My family gave me a unique perspective on life and on this world, and for that I am grateful. My parents, Warren and Janet Ritz, gave me the foundation upon which I built my life. Thank you for allowing me the freedom to explore and make my own choices.

My siblings, Sue Edwards, Greg Ritz, Kathy Hyland, Tracy Logan, and Andrew Ritz, provided me with many opportunities for practicing all of the values introduced to us growing up. Together, we learned that flipping over the top of the swing set is not a good idea, there are better ways to get your vegetables than eating chocolate sauerkraut cake, and positive communication is a challenge when all eight of us are stuffed into a station wagon for twelve hours during our summer road trips! Sharing bedrooms, waiting in line for the bathroom, and a love of goofing around gave us lots of time to practice teamwork, problem-solving, and trust. Thanks for a fun ride!

Marianne Stanley, my fellow peace advocate, mentor, and friend, thank you for having a vision of my potential, and for helping me become a better writer. Your encouragement, support, and humor are much appreciated!

Paul K. Chappell, I'm grateful that you opened my eyes to a new way of seeing the world today and tomorrow. You provided a spark that made me want to be more proactive in making a positive change in the world.

Patrick Snow, thank you for being my publishing coach and believing that I am unstoppable! Your knowledge is immense and your positive energy is contagious!

Tyler Tichelaar, my editor, and Shiloh Schroeder, my cover and interior layout designer, thank you for your attention to detail and original ideas that culminated in the book I hold in my hands. It has been a pleasure going on this journey with you.

★ Contents ★

My Journey in Early Education

★

When I was a teenager, I had my first realization that children learn what they see and what they are taught, even unintentionally. Sasha was a toddler I would watch occasionally in the evenings or on the weekends. We would play with toys, chase each other, and play silly interactive games, snuggle, and laugh together. On one occasion, I was talking to her parents, gesturing to emphasize a point, when they each suddenly exclaimed, "That's who she learned that from!" I was amazed, and actually a little stunned, that a simple thing like a gesture could be learned and copied by such a tiny person without trying to teach it to her! It made me realize how important it is to have qualified teachers around our youngest learners. I decided then and there to become an early childhood educator.

I studied at the University of Illinois where I received my B.S. Degree in Human Development & Family Ecology in 1988. This is a very long name for a degree in child development and family studies with an emphasis on children from birth to five. Upon graduation, I relocated to Rockford, Illinois where I began my teaching career in a birth to three special needs classroom. As a young teacher, I was focused solely on what was happening inside the walls of my classroom. Since I did not see the children at their homes or in the community, it was easy to forget they had another dimension to their lives that I was capable of affecting. So I concentrated on classroom issues: Were the children meeting developmental milestones in the classroom? Were they interacting with each other appropriately? Were they having fun while doing so?

As I gained expertise and became more confident in my teaching abilities, I began to understand the truly unique experience each child had not only while he was in my classroom, but in his world as well. Family and community culture began to become more important to me, and I began to strive to respect each family's unique needs and perspectives both in and out of school. I made an effort to bring their culture and traditions into the classroom in an authentic way.

Soon, extra opportunities began to present themselves to me at work in addition to my teaching responsibilities. I became the assistant director of the day care center and I licensed day care homes to provide another childcare option for the parents of our special needs children. Eventually, I stopped teaching and became a full-time Inclusion and Behavior Specialist for a tri-county area. I was grateful for this chance to visit and learn from so many different childcare programs and the wonderful teachers who worked day in and day out with young children. I learned the important lesson that there is more than one way to run a successful classroom, and that success is reached when individual teachers are able to respect the diverse needs and interests of the children in their care and the teachers are able to bring their unique talents and passions into the mix.

Eight years into my career, my personal life took a dramatic detour. While on vacation in Germany, I met my husband, a fellow American who was working for an aerospace company in Berlin. A year and a half later, I moved to Berlin, Germany. I was newly married, had a sweet five-year-old stepdaughter with me part of the year, and the chance to live in a different and interesting culture. I was excited about the abundant possibilities to travel to new countries and learn about places I had only read about in books or seen in movies. I was not expecting to be able to work during the few years I was overseas with my new family due to work restrictions on Americans at the time.

Opportunity, however, knocked and I found myself directing Berlin's American Embassy Association's Child Care Program. The American Embassy was still not fully staffed in Berlin; after World War II the capital had moved to Bonn and now that East and West Germany were reunited, it was in the process of transitioning back to Berlin. Thus, our program was open to anyone interested in having an American preschool experience.

The chance to live and work in the Early Childhood Education field while living overseas made an enormous impression on me. Not only did I have the unique opportunity to interact with families and teachers from a variety of cultures (American, German, Russian, Italian, Australian, and Canadian, to name a few), but I also had to clarify my definition of what an "American-style" early childhood program could and should provide for its young members.

I discovered that certain values were very important to me. Values about how people treat each other, their belongings, our world. Values about how we view and treat our own bodies and minds. Essentially, I wanted to teach young children to be considerate, kind, compassionate, peaceful, respectful, focused, busy, and happy explorers—to become children aware of their emotions and able to express them appropriately in addition to listening to another person's point of view, and to become children who are interested in solving problems and not frightened of trying. I believed if the children in my care developed these qualities, they would naturally be capable of learning and reaching their developmental potentials, of achieving the educational standards that they are measured against in school.

When it was time to return to the States, I moved to San Diego. I struggled with some of the changes that seemed to have occurred in child care while I was in Germany. There seemed to be a focus on trying to make the childcare experience more like attending elementary school. The shift away from time to explore freely and learn through play appeared to conflict with teaching the values to children that I held so dear. As a program director of a private school, I found this balance became my largest challenge.

When I moved to Seattle, I knew I wanted to get back in the classroom and work on developing these skills on the ground floor. I was extremely fortunate to find an early childhood program that would allow me the freedom to develop my own curriculum as I met the needs of the individual children in my classroom. For almost seven years, I worked primarily in a mixed-age pre-K program. Along with a creative co-teacher, I worked full days with eighteen to twenty children, ages three to five.

While using an emergent curriculum model in the classroom, I was able to balance the children's current interests with the various important lessons related to values that today's children in particular need in order to grow up safely and confidently into the responsible citizens of tomorrow.

After attending a Peace Leadership Training by the Nuclear Age Peace Foundation, I was inspired to begin working as a peace advocate as well. In August 2012, I launched my blog "Nurtured Children Grow. Growing Our Future. One Child at a Time" (http://nurturedchildrengrow. com). Shortly after, I wrote *Empowering the Children: 12 Universal Values Your Child Must Learn To Succeed in Life*. I now offer coaching services to parents and teachers who are interested in empowering the children in their lives.

Introduction

NURTURED KIDS GROW

Nonstop learners,
Understanding and capable leaders,
Rulers with peaceful ways.
Tactful and honest speakers with
Unequaled compassion,
Responding to earth's cries for help.
Empathetic friends who
Debate for and defend the powerless.

Kind and brave contributors,
Inspired innovators.
Devoted and capable
Solvers of humanity's problems.

Generous nonviolent people
Respectfully rooted to the earth.
Our open-minded pathfinders
Waging world peace.

       - Karen Szillat, August 5, 2012

I have always had an affinity for children. They seem to have an openness to life, a joy of living, and a desire to be a part of the world around them. I absolutely admire those qualities, and perhaps I have even hoped that a bit of their positive energy would rub off on me as a parent and teacher, allowing me to do my best in return for them. But I also know that children react to the environment they are in—the words others use, the social climate, the expectations of others; these all play a part in how our children grow and learn. In other words, what we say and do can make it easier or more difficult for our children to be successful in life.

Are you like most parents who are tired at the end of the day, unsure whether what you are doing is effectively helping your children? Do you feel like you are being pulled in many directions and don't know exactly what to focus on to help your children thrive in today's world? Are you concerned about educating your children in our current school system, wondering whether what they are learning is what will ultimately help them become successful members of society? Do you have more than one child to raise, which is a daunting enterprise in itself? Are you a classroom teacher who spends more time focusing on social, emotional, and behavioral skills, leaving you feeling like you don't have enough time to spend on the required educational programming?

When I talk to parents, they readily express these very concerns. Teachers of all ages face these same dilemmas. Many shared concerns exist, with little time to work on every individual problem, and often with few opportunities for collaboration. It is a difficult situation for everyone involved.

When I was growing up in a small town in Illinois, the world was greatly different from how it is today. It seemed to be a simpler time, perhaps because I lived in a rural community, but also because technology has changed dramatically since then. We did not even have cable TV until I was about ten or eleven years old. The only video games I was exposed to were the occasional pinball machine, Pac-Man, or Pong. My five brothers and sisters and I rode bikes, walked all over town with our friends, and learned the skills of negotiation out of necessity. We had only one shower, we shared bedrooms, we squeezed next to each other on picnic benches at the kitchen table, and we all had to fit in one vehicle during car vacations. Teamwork was a necessity.

Writing about it here, it sounds a bit idyllic, and it was a lot of fun. But as a child, I also remember sibling fights, Mom and Dad sometimes seeming a bit overwhelmed or angry at the messes and commotion, and general family chaos. We were a regular family.

The regular family of today has technology competing with the outdoors, organized childhood activities beginning years before kindergarten, and kindergarten looking more like first grade than an introduction to our education system. Parents have a lot of advice thrown at them as they go about living their regular lives.

We know regular does not mean easy. However, regular doesn't mean it has to be so hard either. As humans, adults can be tired mentally, emotionally, physically, or all of the above. And we often do not see immediate results for the time and effort we put into teaching and parenting our children. Is there anything we can do to help ourselves out and take off some of the pressure that we and society place upon us?

What if someone could help you to pinpoint a dozen qualities you could invest time and energy into that would bring you positive results in your children? What if someone could lead you through the maze of suggestions out there and help you to empower your children to become the type of people you want them to be now and in the future?

My stepdaughter is now twenty-three years old, but I can still remember worrying about her a lot when she was growing up. Since she spent time in two households, I was concerned about the consistency between homes, the potential differences in goals and values, and the increasingly high expectations of her school programs. Since she was an only child, I worried about her truly being able to understand cooperation, respect for others' time and space, and the meaning of doing without. My husband and I were busy working full-time, plus we moved a number of times. Were we helping or harming our daughter with our choices?

We parents don't have a crystal ball that can see into the future for us. We have to wait to see how the story plays out. I am proud to say my daughter, Michaele, is a wonderful and beautiful human being. She is educated, cares about those less fortunate than she is, and is beginning to make her own mark on the world. Through trial and error as a parent and as an Early Childhood Education professional, I have developed a program to help other parents and teachers who would like to take a simpler path to success with their own children.

During my twenty years of experience in Early Childhood Education as a teacher, consultant, and administrator, I discovered that certain values were very important to me. By working with hundreds of children in Illinois, Wisconsin, Germany, California, and Washington state, I know firsthand how important it is for our children to be able to learn and work together. I want to teach young children to be considerate, kind, compassionate, peaceful, respectful, focused, busy, and happy explorers. I want them to become children who are aware of their emotions and able to express them appropriately in addition to listening to another person's point of view. I want them to become children who are interested in solving problems and not frightened of trying. I believe if the children in our society develop these qualities, they will naturally be capable of learning and reaching their developmental potentials, of achieving the high educational standards that they are measured against in school.

In this book, you will learn twelve universal values that parents across cultures want for their children, whether they live in the U.S., Canada, Europe, Africa, South America, or elsewhere in the world. These are values about how people treat each other, their belongings, and our world. These are values about how people view and treat their own bodies and minds—values that help them become people who can communicate with others and solve problems. If children are empowered to develop these qualities, they will become happy, successful adults who are prepared for the challenges they may encounter, whatever they may be, as children and adults. These universal values include:

- Safety
- Health
- Communication
- Problem-Solving
- Community Building
- Learning About the World
- Respect
- Responsibility
- Courage
- Honesty
- Caring
- Trust

Whether or not you have children yourself, you are a parent to the next generation. If we can only stop thinking of children as individual property and think of them as the next generation, then we can realize we all have a role to play.
– Charlotte Davis Kasl

I understand you may be apprehensive about trying something new or looking at your children in a new way. It can be unsettling when changes occur, and you may feel like you are already doing so much for your family. But I want to assure you that it is okay to feel that way, and we can take it one step at a time. I am confident that by following the guidelines I offer in this book, you will see your children become empowered in their behaviors, wanting to cooperate because it makes sense to them, and saving you time and energy as their confidence soars! They will become more competent in solving their own problems, interested in learning more about the world, and will participate more fully in it. They will be able to trust in themselves and others, communicating respect and caring for others. This is a powerful and healthy way to live!

I would be honored to be your coach, your "partner in play," as you strive to help your children! I am available to work with parents and teachers in this capacity. It is so much easier to be part of a team than to go it alone, and I am happy to help!

Are you ready to empower the children? Good! Let's do it together! I look forward to growing our future together, one child at a time.

— Karen Szillat

WHO IS JESSICA?

I will often refer to Jessica in this book. Who is she? Jessica Higinbotham was my co-teacher for four years in a classroom of eighteen three to five year olds. We would spend each day together in the Trailblazer classroom, teaching, modeling for, learning from, and exploring with these young people. For nine hours a day, five days a week, we were there for each other, very similar to the way parents are there for each other. We would back each other up, enforce the same rules, and enjoy these young minds and souls while respecting each other's personality. For us, teamwork meant working together toward a common goal, bringing our own strengths to the table, and letting the other shine in areas where she excelled. Competition between partners does not thrive in these types of environments, whereas a passion to do better today than we did the day before does. Jessica was a baby when I was in high school, the same age as the little girl who inspired me to go into teaching. As an adult, she brings a joy of learning to the classroom that children can't help but love to be around. I often wonder what I would be like today if I had had the opportunity to learn with Jessica as my teacher when I was little. I actually think the little girl who still lives in me has been able to process some of the lessons Jessica has done with the children, allowing me more completely to realize my calling. Thank you, Jess!

WHAT I KNOW/WHAT I WANT TO KNOW

When I begin discussing a new topic with a group of children, I always find it helpful to ask first what the children already know or think they know about it. This questioning allows me to clear up any misconceptions from the beginning, and it provides me with a good starting point. I can reinforce issues that most children already know while teaching those concepts to first-time learners. Then I can go right into unfamiliar material. This process allows me to avoid the chorus of "I already know that!" Because, as you know, even very young children are happy to tell you when they already know something!

I also write down the children's answers on a piece of paper or white board as the children tell me what they know or what they think they know. Writing down a person's ideas and answers demonstrates respect for their thoughts and ideas while building their attention span and attention to written words. It also reminds me to clarify certain points with individual parents if needed.

Next, I ask the children what they want to know, what they want to learn about. Their answers allow me to personalize the curriculum a bit more so I can keep them interested and engaged in learning. And when learning is happening, there are far fewer behavior issues to deal with! Again, I write down their thoughts and ideas.

Most children learn best when they have a chunk of uninterrupted time to explore materials. Open-ended materials, meaning there is more than one way to use them, offer the best results. These materials allow for a lot of trial and error, finding a variety of potential solutions to a problem, and evaluating what works best in a situation. This kind of play contributes to in-depth functional learning—the kind of learning that sticks with you, that you can recall down the line and apply in a variety of situations.

HOW TO USE THIS BOOK

- Read it from front to back. It is all valuable information and each slice is important to see what the big picture looks like. However, there are lots of suggestions. They are meant as a brainstorming session for you; then you choose what works best for your children at the time. What is best today may be different from what is best three months or a year from now.

- Pick one chapter or topic to focus on. Is there an area that your children are struggling with? Do you want to help your children develop a particular quality more deeply? Begin there.

- Do you want to work on a variety of skill areas over the course of the year? Look at the end of each chapter to see how you and your family can celebrate throughout the year. Choose holidays that appeal to you and your children. Do you like to play games? Take the Million Minute Family Challenge (September 1-December 31) and try to meet the goal of one million minutes playing games together. Do you like to do silly things together? Celebrate Bubble Wrap Appreciation Day (January 28) or Take Your Houseplants for a Walk Day (July 27). If there is a holiday you like but miss the day, celebrate it on a different day! Make up your own unique family specific holidays! Google the holidays if you want more information on specific ones.

- Research shows that it takes twenty-one days to make something a habit. Give yourself time to practice new skills, just like you give your children time to practice and learn. The goal is to add to our toolbox, so we have more tools available to choose from in different situations. No one tool works for every circumstance, just like your hammer will never work to screw something in no matter how skilled you are at hammering!

Chapter One

Safety

★

Prepare and prevent, don't repair and repent.
– Author Unknown

As a freshman in college, I attended a large university in the Midwest on a beautiful campus filled with old buildings, enormous trees, and thousands of students. In fact, there were so many students that it was easy to forget that as pedestrians we needed to look out for cars, bikes, and other forms of transportation. Even though I had been crossing the street by myself since I first walked myself to kindergarten, I needed to rethink this skill once I went away to college. You see, there were many one-way streets on my campus. I wrongly assumed that cars would only drive the correct direction down a one-way street. This was an old lesson I quickly relearned, which came in handy multiple times each week: Look both ways before crossing the street!

The word safety conjures up different images to different people. My friend Marianne, who is a college professor, immediately thinks of freedom to express your thoughts and ideas without fear of retribution; this is a type of intellectual safety. My husband, on the other hand, links safety with images of freedom from crime. The dictionary defines safety as 1. the state of being safe; freedom from the occurrence or risk of injury, danger, or loss. 2. the quality of averting or not causing injury, danger, or loss.

SAFETY FIRST!

If you asked the eighteen children, ages three to five, in my classroom during any given year what our #1 Classroom Rule is, they would all say, "Safety first!" This was not a call for them to be overly worried that danger was lurking around every corner, but rather a vote of confidence that with proper training, *they could become aware* of the types of things that had the potential to harm them or someone else, and then *they could make the best decision possible* to stay safe. In the life of a small child, safety may look like: looking for cars before crossing the street, holding the butter knife by the handle, sitting on your bottom while chewing and swallowing your food, or using "walking feet" in the classroom.

I was very fortunate to work for a number of years with a co-teacher, Jessica Higinbotham, who inspired and motivated me each day to do my best with the children. Although Jessica and I had blanket rules for all the children in our classroom, we also knew that each child needed to be looked at as an individual, and needed to have his or her strengths and weaknesses assessed. This need applies to children in the same family, too. For example, high energy or easily distracted children had limited partner choices for neighborhood walks: holding the hand of a teacher or another child who was a strong positive role model, instead of their best friend who energized them even more. This same technique could be applied with an over-stimulated sibling on a trip to the store. The expectation is that the high energy child will hold the parent's hand instead of walking with the other sibling.

Jessica and I would also begin the new school year by spending a lot of time teaching and practicing the classroom rules. Spending time learning these rules at the beginning of the year, when a new student joined our classroom and when problems arose, allowed for a preventative approach to be utilized. The first few weeks were very intense learning periods, but then our days quickly calmed down as the kids internalized the routine, the rules, and the understanding of why our room functioned the way it did. We told the children that all decisions were based on their safety and providing fun opportunities for each of them to learn.

Jessica and I would inform the children of a rule (after they helped us come up with a list of rules which we would condense into three to five main rules that could apply to all situations in the classroom, playground, hallway, etc.), why we had the rule, and show them how to implement the rule. Then they would practice the rule through games, during play scenarios, and during actual life situations.

- For example, a classroom rule might be to "Keep your feet on the floor." We state it in a positive manner, meaning we tell the kids what *to do* instead of what *not to do*. (Do not say, "No standing on furniture, toys, people, etc."). It isn't always obvious to young kids what we want them to do when we say, "Don't…" Be clear from the beginning with your expectations, or you may quickly find yourself debating with a child who has a great vocabulary that he "didn't throw it," he "smashed it." Time wasted, toys broken, lesson not learned. True story!

- Why do we have this rule? Pick one simple thing to share with your child, based on his or her development, unless he or she wants more information. "Chairs are for sitting." "This chair falls over easily." "I'm worried you might bump your head."

- Time to practice scenarios. Provide a low prop to stand on, asking one child to stand on it. Have the kids practice telling their friends to put their feet on the floor. Switch roles. Or practice being the teacher/parent and child in the same situation.

Notice what happens in actual life, fine tuning the practice situations as needed.

As parents and teachers, we owe it to our kids to allow them to gain self-confidence as they try to stretch themselves, attempting to create and master new skills on the road to independence. But we must do so at the pace each child is ready for and as he or she is capable of progressing to the next step. Lenore Skenazy discusses this topic and expands on it very well in her book *Free-Range Kids: Giving Our Children the Freedom We Had Without Going Nuts with Worry.* She recommends we do it one "mini-lesson" at a time to help children grow their wings. When we let go a little at a time at a pace that makes sense for our individual child, home, or classroom, it also gives us the confidence as parents and teachers to let go a little, trust our children, and trust in the world's goodness.

EMPOWERING THE CHILDREN

What are a few things we can do to help our little ones feel the wind in their hair both literally and figuratively? Take a few baby steps. First, ask your children what they really wish to accomplish and find ways to help them reach their goals. Help yourself by showing your children how to do things you might normally do for them because it is quicker or potentially "safer." With practice, they will become more independent and have the knowledge needed to do tasks safely.

Some more opportunities for young children include:

- Cutting fruit with a butter knife. A popsicle stick works well for two year olds trying to spread jam on their toast. Demonstrate this for them; then let them practice on their own.

- Cleaning up their own messes as they occur, as well as regular maintenance of community areas. This maintenance could include cleaning up spilled juice, washing food off the dinner table or classroom table and chairs, or putting toys away before moving on to the next activity.

- Using tools like a stapler or clothespins that you squeeze. Providing thumbtacks, showing kids how to handle them, use them, and what to do if they find a stray one, is also a lesson in confidence and safety.

- Showing kids how to be gentle when observing and interacting with wildlife, and then trusting them with the opportunity to practice their skills. This interaction includes animals such as cats, dogs, and birds, but also extends to insects and other creatures. Learning to interact appropriately with wildlife can keep both kids and other living creatures safe. An activity if you do not have a pet could be to have a snail (or slug) circus! Collect a couple of snails or slugs from the garden, placing them gently in a dish tub. Put a piece of rope or string across the tub, securing it with duct or masking tape. Will the snails and slugs "walk the tightrope"? Add leaves for them to eat and a little saucer of water for hydration. Observe their activities by drawing pictures, taking notes, making predictions, and recording results.

- Allowing children to do bigger chores, like setting the entire table, including the breakable dishes. Children can't learn to handle fragile items properly if we never give them the opportunity to practice handling them. Empty glass food jars are a good introduction to fragile items for children to learn with, including what to do if one breaks. Add jars to a dish bin to play with or wash, or give them to your children to place gently in the recycling bin.

- Letting your children play outside at home or the park, allowing them to make friends with other families they meet along the way. Give them a little space to play and maneuver without hovering or worry-ing that someone is going to kidnap them. Rely on other parents to help keep an eye on the children so you can run to the bathroom with your other child, or vice-versa. You might even be able to take turns running errands while the other parent watches your children.

Parents are already great at spreading the word to their kids about things like not picking up broken glass, or not touching the stove. So I'm going to focus on gun safety, fire safety, and water safety. Because of their changing develop-mental insights, growing children require adults to explain clearly messages related to safety again and again in slightly different ways.

If you don't think it's safe, it probably isn't.
– Author Unknown

GUNS AND KIDS: STOPPING OUR FUTURE DEAD IN THEIR TRACKS

"Renee was shot and she died today."

My mom's words faded as my mind raced, trying to grasp the unreality of what she was saying. How could my ten-year-old cousin have died today? Renee, the sweet blond-haired blue-eyed girl who laughed easily and loved drawing pictures? This could not be possible. I had just walked in the door laughing, on one of my first days of high school. The sun was shining brightly and the birds were singing, yet my insides were being shredded as I stood there in the kitchen doorway.

I still think repeatedly about this awful day and the devastation it brought my family, even though it was over thirty years ago. My cousin was at the babysitter's house, and the kids found a gun. Because the kids didn't know what to do in this kind of situation, it ended in tragedy.

The devastation was far-reaching and Renee's abrupt death had a huge impact on my extended family. Renee never had the chance to grow up, to go to a school dance, to graduate from high school, to get married, or to have a family of her own. I struggled with wishing I had died instead of my very young cousin, even though I was only a child myself. I was very sad and angry about the destruction to my family, especially because it was entirely avoidable.

Federal statistics show that guns are in almost half of all U.S. households. So even if you do not have a gun in your home, it is very likely that your children will come in contact with a gun elsewhere. Would your children know what to do if they saw a gun at their grandparents' house? At a friend's house? Thrown under a bush at the park?

Regardless of politics, kids and guns don't mix. Once a trigger is pulled, the effect of the bullet can never be taken back. A simple way to explain this to children is to try the Toothpaste Experiment. Have you ever squeezed all of the toothpaste out of a toothpaste tube? And then tried to put the toothpaste back in the tube? Once the toothpaste is out of the tube, there is no way to put it back again. That is how it is with shooting a gun at a person. The devastation is done and you can't make it the way it was again, no matter how hard you try.

Serious discussions must occur in every house between parents and their children as soon as the children begin to show interest in gun play or they see weapons on TV or in the house. This discussion could be held as early as three years of age. There is a great resource available to parents and educators for children in pre-K through third grade that simply promotes the prevention of gun accidents. The NRA's Eddie Eagle GunSafe Program materials can usually be acquired free of charge through grant funding. They include a DVD, parent brochures, student workbooks, posters, stickers, and coins with Eddie Eagle's important safety steps on them. Check out their website www.nrahq.org/safety/eddie or call (800)231-0752.

In honor of Renee, I made sure to discuss gun safety with the children and parents I've had the pleasure to work with over the years. Using the resources from Eddie Eagle were very helpful because his message is clear and easy to remember: "STOP! Don't Touch. Leave the Area. Tell an Adult." I have often heard the children in my class singing this jingle on the playground or in the classroom during play. Overheard conversations included, "Grandma, I found a gun in the closet!" and "Someone call 911! There is a gun in the park!" My co-teacher and I noticed that play changed from trying to "shoot and capture bad guys" to "teaching people who needed to learn a better way."

One day, the grandfather of a little boy, whom I will call Jacob, stopped to thank me because he had never thought about discussing guns with his grandson, thinking he was too young. The grandfather told me he was a gun owner and decided to test his five-year-old grandson. He put his unloaded gun in a desk drawer that Jacob often explored while searching for drawing supplies. He asked Jacob to get him a pen, and when Jacob opened the drawer and saw the gun, Jacob ran to the sofa and said, "Look out! A gun! Don't touch!" The grandfather had tears in his eyes as he proudly relayed his story to me.

EMPOWERING THE CHILDREN

As a teacher, I also take the time to ask the kids questions to help them think more deeply about possible scenarios they might encounter in the real world:

- What if the gun looks like a toy or your friend tells you it is a toy? Do you play with it?

- What if you are at your favorite aunt's house, your aunt who loves you so much and would never hurt you? Is it okay to touch a gun you find at her house?

- What if your best friend says he won't be your friend anymore if you don't hold the gun?

- What is the difference between a real gun and a toy gun? Can you always tell just by looking?

I find that asking such questions opens the door to more questions, allowing me to understand better what my young friends understand from their perspectives. In addition, I write down their thoughts, concerns, and questions on a piece of paper or white board to share with their parents so they have access to as much of the conversation as possible.

You might be a firefighter if your kids are afraid
to get into water fights with you.
– Author Unknown

A KID'S GUIDE TO FIREFIGHTING

"I want to be a firefighter!" How many times have you heard this phrase from a young child or even said it yourself when you were little? Firefighters are some of today's real life superheroes, who come racing to the rescue on fast red trucks, sirens blaring, to the relief of everyone in sight. Adults call them when they have a fire emergency, and they show up when there is a car accident or medical emergency. They wear cool uniforms and get to slide down fire poles. Firefighters have a lot of appeal for young children, so it naturally follows that fires also attract the attention of kids.

There are many lessons to teach children about fires besides "Fire is hot" or "Don't touch!" I am reminded of this every October during Fire Prevention Month, as well as each time the newspaper headlines are discussing wildfires that tend to destroy homes and attract many firefighters and other volunteers to local communities. What do we tell our children about local disasters or similar ones that they may hear about on TV or through adult discussions, or see pictures of in newspapers, magazines, or on the computer?

Often, adults are reluctant to discuss potentially disturbing topics because they want to protect their children from worry, keep them innocent for as long as possible, or are unsure of what to say. While I do not profess to have all of the answers, I do know from personal experience that children have creative imaginations and can come up with their own scary versions of reality. Partial knowledge coupled with a child's imagination in instances like a fire can create confusion, despair, nightmares, and problem behaviors. Children are not always capable of asking the "right" questions, and depending on their ages, they often show their distress in their behaviors.

I also like to act from a preventative point of view, clear up misconceptions, educate, and allow children to ask questions and explore topics more deeply. For example, most deaths in a house fire occur from smoke inhalation, not burns. Young children often mistakenly believe they can hide from the smoke under their blankets, or find safety under their beds or in their closets. They need to be told that the safe place to be is outside where there is fresh air.

Most children learn best when they have a block of continuous time to investigate materials. Materials that are open-ended, meaning there is more than one way to use them, are very successful in this task. They allow for a lot of trial and error, finding a variety of promising results to a dilemma, and deciding what solution works. This kind of play contributes to comprehensive functional learning. This is the kind of learning that endures, that you can bring to mind when needed, and apply in new situations.

EMPOWERING THE CHILDREN

Below is my plan to help children learn about issues related to firefighting and fire safety, specifically as it related to some wildfires in Cle Elum, Washington in August 2012. You may notice this is a lengthy section. Does this mean a parent or teacher is expected to touch upon every item or that this topic is the most important of the safety topics? No. Simply use it as a template for any number of topics that are important for you to address with your children. Focus on what the kids do not know. Focus on what concerns them or what concerns you the most; after all, you know your children better than anyone else knows them.

AFTER FINDING OUT WHAT THE CHILDREN KNOW AND WHAT THEY WANT TO KNOW (See box in the Introduction for more discussion of this concept), TELL THE KIDS ABOUT THE SPECIAL PROBLEM HAPPENING RIGHT NOW, THE FIRE IN THE CLE ELUM AREA. HOUSES AND THE FOREST ARE ON FIRE.	
Ideas to Explore	Sample Activities
• Location of fires. • Use of maps. • Are we in a safe location?	• Show the kids on a map where the fire is and where we are located to assure them of their safety. • Help find ways to relate the distance to them, such as, "If you were in the car for a long time, like from morning snack until lunchtime, that is how long it would take to drive to the fire from school."

HOW DO YOU THINK THIS FIRE STARTED? IT WAS NEAR A LOT OF TREES, HOUSES, AND MEN WORKING ON A ROAD.	
Ideas to Explore	Sample Activities
• Possible causes of fires. • What clues would some-one follow to figure out what started the fire?	• Provide materials in the block area for kids to act out scenarios: toy firefight-ers, straws/hoses, "paper fire" (cut or tear red, or-ange and yellow flames out of paper; can be laminated for repeated use or to spray with water), fire station, emergency vehicles, fire trucks, houses. • Provide materials in the dramatic play area for kids to act out scenarios: boots, jackets, hats, garden hoses, badges, oxygen tanks (milk jugs or soda bottles with tubes attached that kids can wear on their backs), emergency vehicles or fire trucks made from card-board boxes, cardboard houses, paper fire, tele-phones, walkie-talkies (real ones or make from small cardboard boxes or scraps), construction hats, tools.

HOW DO YOU THINK THE FIREFIGHTERS KNEW TO COME?	
Ideas to Explore	**Sample Activities**
• Signs of a fire: smoke, flames, funny smell. • Calling 911.	• Provide pictures of phones with children's phone numbers written on them; practice dialing phone number and 911. • Use real cell phones to practice turning phone on/off and dialing 911 (no battery in them please!). • Practice telling 911 operator what your emergency is.

WHY DO FORESTS BURN?	
Ideas to Explore	Sample Activities
• Too much brush and overgrowth. • Too much close construction. • Lack of controlled burns. • Too much close construction. • Lightning. • Dry conditions. • Damaged trees (insects and disease).	• Utilize books such as: • *Wildfires* by Seymour Simon • *Fire in Their Eyes: Wildfires and the People Who Fight Them* by Karen Magnuson Beil • *Contain the Flame: Outdoor Fire Safety (How to Be Safe!)* by Jill Urban Donahue

IS IT ALWAYS BAD FOR FORESTS TO BURN?	
Ideas to Explore	Sample Activities
• Release of seeds. • Replenishment of nutrients to soil.	• Provide pine cones to explore, cut open.

WHAT HAPPENS TO A BODY WHEN THERE IS A FIRE?	
Ideas to Explore	Sample Activities
• Smoke inhalation is biggest danger. Can't breathe. • Never hide under bed or blankets. • Always go with firefighter even if scared. • Leave your snuggle buddy and blanket. Objects can be replaced; people cannot be replaced.	• Arrange an assortment of items (toys, clothes, household items, etc.) in front of the kids. Ask them, "Can this object be replaced if it is damaged or destroyed?" Help the kids to realize that if an object or item can be bought at a store or a new one can be made, then they must not spend time collecting it during a fire. Reinforce to the children that their only job is to leave the house and go to the family meeting spot.

WHAT DO FIREFIGHTERS LOOK AND SOUND LIKE?	
Ideas to Explore	**Sample Activities**
• What if it is dark and smoky? • What if the firefighter has an oxygen mask on and talks (sounds like Darth Vader)?	• Get fire safety DVD from local fire department. • Visit a fire department or have firemen visit your school.

WHAT WOULD YOU DO IF THERE WERE A FIRE IN YOUR HOUSE?	
Ideas to Explore	Sample Activities
• Two evacuation plans per location (home, school, grandparents' house). • Stop, drop, and roll. • Crawl under smoke. • Practice fire (earthquake and tornado) drills. • Calling 911. • Batteries in smoke detectors.	• Practice "Stop, drop, and roll." • Crawl low under "smoke" (sheet hung low in room or crawl under the length of a table). • Decide whether you should "Keep away" from objects or whether objects are "Safe for play." • Find paper fires hidden in classroom and extinguish them with hoses. • Make a fire escape plan at school and at home. • Practice calling 911. • Practice fire drills. • Count smoke detectors at home.

WHAT DO FIREFIGHTERS NEED TO DO TO BE PREPARED?	
Ideas to Explore	**Sample Activities**
• Healthy diet. • Exercise for strength and endurance. • Team player. • Never go in to fight fires alone. • Study building plans and area maps.	• Draw fire escape plans and maps for home and school. • Have a fire safety inspection tour of home and school. • Arrange a "rescue the stuffed animal" obstacle course (counting to make sure you did not leave any animals behind!). • Play fire rescue outside with hoses (use two hands or two-plus firefighters per hose), buckets, and wagons. • Have a bucket brigade. (Pass bucket of water down the line without spilling!) • Practice a firefighter's workout. • Prepare and eat a meal together, just like firefighters who stay all day and night at the firehouse. Make sure the meal includes muscle-building protein. • Search the classroom for hidden paper fires and paper smoke.

WHAT HAPPENS IN A HOUSE WHEN THERE IS A FIRE?	
Ideas to Explore	Sample Activities
• Smoke. • Flames. • Hot handles on doors.	• Practice crawling low under "smoke" (sheet hung low in room or crawl under the length of a table). • Practice touching a closed door to decide whether or not it feels hot. • If the door feels hot, there is most likely fire on the other side and the door should remain closed. • If the door feels hot and must remain closed, practice finding an alternative exit. • If the door must remain closed and there is not an alternative exit, practice placing a rolled up wet towel under the door to keep the smoke from entering the room.

The door to safety swings on the hinges
of common sense.
– Author Unknown

WATER SAFETY ISSUES

I can remember loving to splash in the pool as a young girl. I took swimming lessons, but I never really had the opportunity to swim very much in our overcrowded community pool. Feeling overly confident my first time at a lake, I didn't realize how far it was back to the shore after swimming with my cousin out toward the middle. Neither did he. As he started to go under water for the third time, another older cousin finally heard his weak call for help. We were very lucky that day.

EMPOWERING THE CHILDREN

Years later, I was a teacher at a special needs day care that was fortunate enough to take the toddlers for pool time at the local YMCA. I was so impressed because the primary thing the instructors were teaching these little ones was how to pull themselves out of the pool and to indicate whether they were too tired to stay in the water. What a great lesson! I had never even thought about this as an elementary school child or even young teenager. Yet children who were developmentally at the level of a toddler could signal with words, sounds, or actions that they needed out for a rest once they were taught this lesson!

What other things are good to teach your child about water?

- Always go with a grown-up. Never swim alone.
- Just because you can swim does not mean you don't need a life vest in certain situations. It helps you to float and is important for the following reasons:
  - You could fall out of a boat unexpectedly.
  - There are waves in the water.
  - A lot of other people are in the water, making it difficult to see you.

- There is a current in the water; you are in a lake, river, ocean.

- The water is so cold it can cramp your muscles.

- Goggles help keep the salt, chlorine, or chemicals in the water out of your eyes.

- When you calm your mind, it calms your body. When you calm your body, it calms your mind.

- If you are tired, take a break.

- If you go out from the shore, from the boat, or from the edge of the pool, you have to get back again.

SUMMARY

Please do all you can to protect our future, our collective children.

- If you decide to have a gun in your home, the only responsible option is to have the unloaded gun locked up, safely secured away from curious children. And please talk to your children about guns now. Check out the Eddie Eagle GunSafe Program. Squeeze some toothpaste together. Then hug each other.

- Have a plan for evacuation in case of a fire at home and school. Add tornado and earthquake drills if these are appropriate for your locale.

- Review water safety with children.

- Remember, as children's brains grow and develop, their understanding of danger, safety, and their own abilities changes. Review safety issues at least as often as you would change the batteries in your smoke detector, which is twice a year.

CELEBRATING SAFETY THROUGHOUT THE YEAR

★

January: Backward Day (31)

February: Boy Scout Day (8)

March: American Red Cross Month

                Poison Prevention Awareness Month

April: Medication Safety Week (First week)

                Pet First Aid Awareness Month

May: Recreational Water Illness & Injury
                Prevention Week (Week before
                Memorial Day)

                National Learn to Swim Day (18)

                National Safe Boating Week (Third week)

June: National Gun Safety Month

                Fireworks Safety Month

                Home Safety Month

                National Safety Month

                School Safety Month

July: Fireworks Safety Month

                National Make a Difference to
                Children Month

August: Children's Eye Health and Safety Month

September:	Emergency Care Month
October:	Baby Safety Month
	Sports Eye Safety Month
	National Preparedness Month
October:	Fire Prevention Month
	National Crime Prevention Month
	Animal Safety and Protection Month
	National Bullying Prevention Month
	Drive Safely to Work Week (First week)
November:	Marooned Without a Compass Day (6)
December:	Safe Toys & Gifts Month

Chapter Two

Health

★

Just because you're not sick doesn't
mean you're healthy.
– Author Unknown

We've already looked at the importance of safety in the life of a child. After all, if we don't have safety first, how can we focus on building the rest of our strong foundation for our children to grow from, to set down roots, and to allow their branches to reach toward the sky?

The next crucial building block is health. Not only do we need to provide our children with the food, exercise, and medicine to be healthy, but we also want to provide them with the skills to make good choices about their mental and physical health. By teaching young children why sleep, nutrition, and exercise are important, by demonstrating stress reduction techniques with them and showing them how to cope with loss, by emphasizing the importance of preventative medical care, we intend to raise children who can cope with the ups and downs of life in positive ways.

PHYSICAL HEALTH

When I was growing up, my brothers and sisters and I spent the bulk of our time playing outside. Riding bikes, playing tag, jumping in the leaves, and climbing on the swing set. We also would go to parks, wander around our small town, and walk to and from school. Exercise was built into our days through play at home and PE classes at school, and as we got into junior high and high school, participating on sports teams became more important as well.

Today's young children have a much different experience. Organized sports often begin long before kindergarten, with parents driving their children to events from pre-k through high school. The focus is on competitive games with winners and losers. Open-ended playtime is less prevalent today, especially outdoors. Most children spend thirty-two or more hours a week watching TV or playing video games.[1] As a result of this sedentary lifestyle, childhood obesity is a real concern.

EMPOWERING THE CHILDREN

With this change, we must look at a new way to teach children to use their bodies as well. In our high stress world with the pressure to succeed in sports and school, we need to learn stress reduction techniques. Here are a few techniques that will work for you!

1 McDonough, P. "TV viewing among kids at an eight-year high." Nielsenwire. October 26, 2009. Available at: http://blog.nielsen.com/ nielsenwire/media_entertainment/tv-viewing-among-kids-at-an-eight-year-high/. Accessed October 25, 2012.

- Tai Chi is one way to teach children to become aware of their breath. As they breathe in and out consciously, they learn to focus, relax, and calm their bodies. Tai Chi can also teach children the value of balance, flow, and moving *with* as opposed to *against* conflict.

- Progressive relaxation involves relaxing one body part at a time by squeezing the muscles and then relaxing them, beginning with your feet and moving up the entire body.

- Meditative storytelling refers to listening to a story while the eyes are closed.

  ▸ The children I've worked with appeared to enjoy Tai Chi, progressive relaxation, and meditative storytelling during school. We would participate in it when "things were getting crazy" as a nice break as well as part of our pre-lunch/pre-nap routine. Some children described their experiences like this:

    ▸▸ I feel soft. Like when I'm under the covers.

    ▸▸ I feel good and sometimes sad. I have feelings.

    ▸▸ I feel really melted. I feel warm and toasty.

    ▸▸ I feel really good. And how I feel when I pet my dog.

    ▸▸ It feels like a warm bath, so cozy and good.

    ▸▸ It makes me want to go to bed and go to sleep.

  ▸ When: Before bedtime, when stressed, upset, or overstimulated.

- ▸ Recommended Resources:

  - ▸▸ *Peaceful Piggy Meditation* by Kerry Lee MacLean

  - ▸▸ *Tai Chi for Kids: Move Like the Animals* by Stuart Alve Olson

  - ▸▸ *The Power of Relaxation: Using Tai Chi and Visualization to Reduce Children's Stress* by Patrice Thomas

- Yoga can also be beneficial to children's stress relief. Again, children learn awareness of their breath and then can slow it. This process is calming to the body.

  - ▸ The candle is a pose done often in our room as a group or when a child needs help calming down. Simply put your palms together, close your eyes, and slowly breathe in and out three times, or the number of years your child is old.

  - ▸ A similar activity using the breath to calm down the self is to direct the children to "Smell the flower; blow it out."

  - ▸ Children usually love animals and yoga poses can be named after animals. Children also enjoy imitating poses and trying a variety of physical challenges. Yoga is great for these reasons.

    Recommended Resources:

    - ▸▸ *The ABCs of Yoga for Kids* by Teresa Anne Power

    - ▸▸ *Yoga Kit for Kids Fun and Fitness* by Imaginazium

NUTRITION

Specific nutrition advice is beyond the scope of this book. A pediatrician or nutritionist is the best source for that. I can, however, provide you with ways to empower children to make wise nutrition choices.

EMPOWERING THE CHILDREN

- Help your children become aware of the effects different kinds of foods have on their systems. Ask them how they feel after they eat a certain food? Tired? Energized? Hungry? Full?

- "Eat the Alphabet" with your children by trying new foods that begin with each letter of the alphabet. The only rules: Adults and children must try a mouse-size bite! If they do not like the food, they must say so politely. For example, "No thank you; I don't care for this." Be a good role model when you dislike a food, too! Keep in mind that it may take trying a food fifteen times before a child likes a new food, so do not give up too soon! Try foods in different forms, such as raw, cooked, or in a smoothie. Side note: I personally never cared for fish, but I was able to train my taste buds by eating a little fish every day for two weeks.

- Tell stories to your children about how you didn't like a food at first but changed your mind after you tried it once or twice, or how you thought you wouldn't like a food but did like it after you tried it.

- "Eat the Rainbow" with your children. Discuss the benefits of eating a variety of foods every day: red, orange, yellow, green, blue, indigo, and violet. Each color gives your body different nutrients, so all are necessary for optimal health.

- Eat at least five fruits and vegetables a day. Empower your children by having them help choose which ones they are going to eat that day.

- Compare ingredients in popular processed treats to whole foods. For example, our school cook came to our classroom with a box of strawberry roll-ups. She read the ingredients to the children, who were as surprised as I was to find out there were no strawberries in the strawberry roll-ups! We then gathered ingredients to make our own roll-ups with real strawberries and other whole foods. Am I saying we should never rely on convenience foods? No, but it can only help children to teach them there is a nutritional difference in the foods they choose to eat. These choices lead to differences in their daily functioning and their short-term and long-term health.

SLEEP

Sleep is an extremely important ingredient in the life of successful children, but its benefits have often been overlooked. Most adults realize a good night's sleep is important for children, but they don't realize that researchers are finding sleep to be as important to functioning as nutrition, hydration, or safety. Our lives get busy so it is easy to let bedtime routines fall to the wayside or not to have one to begin with.

According to Marc Weissbluth, MD, author of *Healthy Sleep Habits, Happy Child,* "Sleep is the power source that keeps your mind alert and calm. Every night and at every nap, sleep recharges the brain's battery. Sleeping well increases brainpower just as weight lifting builds stronger muscles, because sleeping well increases your attention span and allows you to be physically relaxed and mentally alert at the same time. Then you are at your personal best." In order for children to function their best at school, at home, and anywhere else they may spend their time, sleep allows them to be alert, calm, and have a long attention span. These benefits in turn lead them to be optimal learners.

What do we need to know about sleep?

- Kids need to have the right amount of sleep for their bodies to grow and develop to their best ability. Otherwise, they can't function optimally. How much sleep do most individuals require? While sleep requirements vary by individual, the National Institute of Neurological Disorders and Stroke reports that most adults need seven to eight hours a night, though some people may need as few as five hours per night and others may need up to nine or ten hours of sleep each day for proper functioning.

  ▸ Sleep Requirements by Age

    ▸▸ Newborns (0-2 months old) 12-18 hours

    ▸▸ Infants (3-11 months) 14-15 hours

    ▸▸ Toddlers (1-3 years) 12-14 hours

    ▸▸ Pre-schoolers (3-5 years old) 11-13 hours

    ▸▸ School-aged kids (5-10 years) 10-11 hours

    ▸▸ Teens (11-17 years) 8-9 hours

    ▸▸ Adults 7-9 hours

- In order for proper development of the nervous system, sleep must be of sufficient length and quality to allow for participation in all levels of sleep.

- Naps are important in your children's development because the type of sleep is different than the sleep your children get during the night. Napping has an effect on your children's alertness, and while napping, the brain organizes the learning that your children have participated in prior to sleep.

- Sleeping at night and during nap time is most restorative when it aligns with your children's rhythm. It is more important to align your schedule with your children's than vice versa.

- Sleep problems at night cause problems during the day, too. Kids can be more disruptive, emotional, distracted, impulsive, inattentive, less alert, and less able to concentrate at school and at home.

- Even a little less sleep can have an impact on your children. The change in adrenaline levels that occurs when your children are tired may make them appear wide-awake. Instead of putting them to bed later, you might find that putting your hyped-up children to bed fifteen minutes earlier actually works better.

- Kids who score A's in school tend to get thirty minutes more sleep per night than those who score D's.

- Sleep problems can affect a child's I.Q. as negatively as lead exposure, according to Paul Suratt of the University of Virginia.

- Kids who slept a single hour less than they needed increased their risk of obesity by 80 percent. This result is because the hormones that control hunger are directly related to sleep quality; with too little rest, your children's appetite turns itself on and stays on.[2]

EMPOWERING THE CHILDREN

To help your children learn how to make sleep work for them, try some of the following activities:

- Have quiet activities in the home an hour before bedtime begins. Puzzles, books, and drawing are all calming and help transition to a relaxing sleep time.

- Explain the benefits of sleep to your children. It is motivating for them to know they are helping their bodies and brains grow and learn while they sleep! Help them think of specific goals they would like to reach, such as touching the branch of the tree when they jump, understanding a math problem at school, or playing with friends or siblings without arguing. Explain how sleep will help them achieve their goals.

- Limit distractions in the bedroom. Use blackout curtains to make the room darker if needed. Use a sound machine to mask noises in other areas of the house or outside. Do not allow TVs, computers, or telephones in the bedroom.

- Have a consistent, predictable bedtime routine and regular bedtime every night, even on weekends. Otherwise,

2 http://children.webmd.com/features/good-sound-sleep-for-children?page=2&print=true. Accessed December 12, 2012.

you will have to fight constantly as you try to readjust to the routine. You can empower your children to take some responsibility for achieving what needs to be done before lights out. Even three year olds can follow a picture board with their routine displayed. Make sure you give them enough time to complete their tasks (pajamas on, teeth brushed, books chosen, toys put away) in any order they see fit.

Making and Using a Picture Board

- Take and print photos of your children doing the items you want them to do.
- Alternatives:
  - ▸ Draw pictures of your children completing desired tasks.
  - ▸ Have your children draw pictures of themselves completing desired tasks.
  - ▸ Write a list of "To Do" items.
- Attach pictures/list to a posterboard.
- Add a small square or circle next to the picture.
- Cover with clear contact paper.
- Provide a dry erase marker for the children to mark next to the box that they have completed the items.

- Provide at least thirty minutes of a "wind down" activity, such as story-time for younger children, or a hot, relaxing bath for older kids.

- Give them some "sleeping potion" to use on themselves or their wiggly snuggle buddy. A sleeping potion can be simply a pinch of magic sprinkles or mini-confetti that calms the mind and body that you keep in a special bag or bottle. A sleeping potion worked well at nap-time for my students, but I had to add a dose of reality by saying I could purchase it at Costco; otherwise, even the little ones were too skeptical to believe!

- Use a spritz of lavender essential oil in a mist of water to help kids calm down by spraying it on their pajamas, pillowcases, or snuggle buddies. Diffusers also work well with essential oils.

- Utilize a technique called "swimming stuffies." Put a snuggle buddy on your child's chest. Have your child watch it swim up and down as he or she breathes in and out deeply.

PREVENTATIVE CARE

Parents and teachers understand and remember that we need to help children in their quest for a healthy body. We schedule the required preventative check-ups with pediatricians to make sure our children are developing on target. Part of these doctor visits include discussions about topics to make sure our children are thriving. A few things to consider are included in the section below.

EMPOWERING THE CHILDREN

- Immunizations: Children who are not immunized frequently contract childhood diseases in college, often with fatal or dramatic effects such as sterility from mumps. Explain to your children why they are receiving their shots. (For example, "The shot will stop you from getting really sick from the mumps now and when you are older. Plus, if you don't get the shot and you get sick when you are older, you will pass the mumps to other kids who didn't get their shots either. If you get mumps when you are older, you get a lot sicker than when you are a kid and you get it.")

- Doctor visits: You can begin to empower your children by helping them to write in their own words what symptoms, concerns, and questions they have for the doctor. To help your children prepare for upcoming appointments, the opportunity for pretend play can be invaluable. Fears, concerns, questions, and confusion about a procedure or situation can come out during play and a variety of solutions can be practiced.

- Dental visits: Dental health is often secondary to medical health in the minds of many adults. Health insurance may not include dental insurance, so it is put in the background until pain forces it into the forefront. However, scientists are discovering more links between dental and cardiac health, in addition to the pain many children suffer due to tooth loss and decay. All children should see a dentist before their first birthday, and a routine of brushing and flossing should be routine as soon as teeth are present. Allow children to hold their own toothbrushes and flossing picks or floss from early on. Adults can always put on the finishing touches. (See Chapter 4 for a story about dental health and the Tooth Fairy.)

- Proper hand-washing is the most important and empowering way to stay healthy!

▸ Teach your children how to wash their hands properly and be a good hand-washing role model for them.

　▸▸ How to wash:

　▸▸ Use running water and lots of rubbing. It is the friction that gets the germs off, not the soap.

　▸▸ Wash from the wrists down, including fronts and backs of hands, between fingers, and fingernails.

　▸▸ Turn off faucet with a disposable towel.

　▸▸ Dry hands.

　▸▸ When to wash:

　　• When your hands are dirty.

　　• After toileting.

　　• After playing outside.

　　• After coughing or sneezing.

　　• Before eating.

　▸▸ Teach your kids to keep their fingers out of their eyes, nose, or mouth.

• Teach your children to cough and sneeze into their elbows instead of their hands, which spreads more germs. A great activity to help teach children about these teeny tiny germs is to tear a piece of paper into tiny bits. Have the paper bits in the palm of your hand; then "Sneeze" into the paper bits, blowing them everywhere. The flying bits of paper can demonstrate how your germs spread to other people and objects. A great book for Pre-K to third graders is *Pigs Make Me Sneeze* by Mo Willems. Humor is one of the best ways to learn about subjects like manners and health!

MENTAL HEALTH

Helping Children Deal With Loss

As adults, we often put on our rose-colored glasses when we reflect back on what it was like to be a child. That is, if we can actually remember! Or else we tend to minimize what children might be going through at the time, thinking or hoping that they will not "get it" or remember enough later of what is really happening today. But there are many things that can impact children and their development, making a long-lasting impression on them, determining how they see the world today, and influencing how they will interact in the world tomorrow. Among these things are issues related to loss.

Loss can come in many forms, some obvious and some not so obvious. Loss can be related to the changes that come with divorce in a family, the loss of family members, pets, and friends through death, illness, and moving, and the loss of a favorite toy or security object through physical loss or outgrowing it, to name a few. As parents and educators, we want to do the best we can for our children. We want to spare them pain if possible. We want them to feel safe. We want to help them to understand the ways of the world without becoming afraid to experience life. We want them to know they can come to us, even though we are flawed and do not have all of the answers. This is a tall order, so where do we start?

As I mentioned in the Introduction, a great place to begin is with what your child knows and what your child wants to know. It is easy to worry about details that children are not asking for or ready for, so let's start with a basic conversation first. Are there misconceptions that need to be cleared up? Then we can find a good starting point to begin adding any new material for the children if it is needed.

I believe it imperative to make the following important point before getting deeper into this or any topic: Please do not feel like you have to have all of the answers to your children's questions on the spot. If you do not know how to answer a question, simply say, "That's an interesting question. I need to think about how to answer that for you," or "I need to look up the answer." By supplying children with answers without letting them see us think about decisions or answers, or without observing us research an answer through books, the Internet, or by asking other people, we neglect to show a valuable problem-solving technique to children. We all love to know the answer and "be right," but it is not always necessary to say the answer without demonstrating how an answer could be found. After all, each day as your children grow older, they will be out in the world more often without adult presence. We want our children to become thoughtful problem-solvers who can handle the stress of everyday life as well as during extraordinary situations.

EMPOWERING THE CHILDREN

Here are a few ideas to help you help children on their journey through the ups and downs of life. They can be adapted for use at both home and school, as well as for a variety of ages.

DIVORCE	
Ideas to Explore	Sample Activities
• What is a family? • Types of families. • What is divorce? • Why do people get divorced? • Explore gender roles (who can cook food, clean, fix broken items, be a helper, etc.) in your house and at school. • Teamwork.	• Chart the numbers of grown-ups, children, and animals who live at each child's house or houses. Are they female or male? Compare and contrast charts to everyone else's charts. • Make sure that all members of the family and classroom are contributing participants. Everyone cleans up his or her own mess and takes some responsibility for the environment, belongings, people, and pets that live in the home or attend the program. • Make sure that all roles or jobs are covered, and not just in stereotypical ways. (Example: Men and boys cook, in addition to women and girls.) • In a divorce, keep adult disagreements separate from the children. Both adults should let the children know how much they are loved and wanted by both parents, and that they are not responsible for the

	change in living arrangements.
	• Provide activities that require more than one person (teamwork!) such as carrying a laundry basket, large boxes, carrying grocery bags, or moving chairs. Thank the children for their help, reminding them that you couldn't have done it without them!
	• Contact your local library for children's book suggestions.

TOY/SECURITY OBJECT: LOST	
Ideas to Explore	Sample Activities
• Why do we have toys, snuggle buddies, blankets, etc.? • How should we take care of our belongings? • Strategies to use when we lose something: ▸ How to look for a lost item. ▸ Saving money to replace an item. ▸ Keeping valuables at home.	• Make a "Missing Blanket" poster and post it. • Ask others "Have you seen my missing blanket?" • Give daily chores/jobs as a part of being a family member or classroom member, without money or rewards for being involved. • Discuss if an item can be made or purchased at a store. This means it can be physically replaced.

ILLNESS: PERSON OR PET	
Ideas to Explore	Sample Activities

• Living vs. nonliving.
 	
• Why do people and animals get sick?
 	
• How do we stay healthy?
 	
• Proper hand-washing techniques: why, how, when, and where.
 	
• Preventative health care, including proper nutrition, exercise, and sleep.
	• Doctor or veterinarian dramatic play:
	
	  ▸ doctor jacket
	
	  ▸ medical bag
	
	  ▸ stethoscopes
	
	  ▸ blood pressure cuffs
	
	  ▸ thermometers
	
	  ▸ shots
	
	  ▸ tiny bottles with "pretend" medicine (confetti)
	
	  ▸ models of body parts
	
	  ▸ medical books and charts
	
	  ▸ clipboards
	
	  ▸ Band-Aids (address labels work well for this)
	
	  ▸ red crayons (draw "injuries" on white address labels to stick on people, stuffed animals, and dolls)
	
	  ▸ stuffed animals and dolls
	
	  ▸ First Aid books
	
	  ▸ notepads & pens for writing prescriptions

	▸ blankets & pillows
	▸ X-rays & a light table (or tape X-rays to window for viewing)
	• Make medical drawings (bones, muscles, blood cells and vessels, etc.). Move each other's bodies to feel muscles and bones, comparing them to the medical drawings.
	• Microscopes with slides, or printouts of microbes, etc.
	• Dolls with soap and water
	• "Spread of Germs" demonstration: Blow glitter or tiny pieces of paper from your hand with a "fake" sneeze or cough.
	• Hand-washing demonstration (include running water, soap, washing ALL parts of the hands [tops, bottoms, between fingers, nails, wrists], turning water off with a paper towel, and throwing towel away).
	• Read *Pigs Make Me Sneeze* by Mo Willems
	• Demonstrate how to cover your coughs and sneezes in your elbow.

DEATH: PERSON OR PET	
Ideas to Explore	Sample Activities
• Living vs. non-living • Living vs. dead • Respect for people and animals • Why do people and animals die?	▸ Sort items or photos of living things (people, animals, plants) vs. non-living objects (crayons, rocks, toys, and robots). I have found that robots are a very tricky thing for children to decide whether or not they are living, especially robots that can speak or walk. Discuss the topic and ask questions such as, "How do you know? How are they alike? How are they different?" ▸ Discuss and ask questions such as, "Now that we know which of these items are alive, how do we know when they are dead? How is a living object, such as a live dog, the same as a dead object, like a dead dog? How are these dogs different from each other?" • Discuss raising animals for food. ▸ Using all body parts (reduce, reuse, recycle) if possible.

    ▸ Killing animals as humanely as possible.

- Learn from dead animal bodies and treat them gently and with respect since they were once alive.

    ▸ Purchase a fish or octopus from a grocery store to explore in science area. Provide ice tray, goggles, gloves. Tongs, tweezers, magnifying glasses, charts of body parts.

    ▸ Have a funeral for a pet that has died. Dig a hole together, paint a rock to mark the grave, say, "Thanks for being my friend."

- Read books such as:

    ▸ *Lifetimes: The Beautiful Way to Explain Death to Children* by Bryan Mellonie and Robert Ingpen

    ▸ *The Dead Bird* by Margaret Wise Brown

    ▸ *The Tenth Good Thing About Barney* by Judith Viorst

MOVING: PERSON OR PET	
Ideas to Explore	Sample Activities
• Maps/locations • Keeping in touch • Writing letters • Phone use • Taking photos or drawing pictures • Reasons why people or pets have to move away.	• Write and send letters or drawings to people who live far away. • Use a map to mark the locations where people who are important to your children live. Mark your family vacation spots. • Mark where the children in your classroom live on a city map, along with a photo of their dwellings and/or addresses. • A child in my class had to give his beloved dachshund to a new family because the dog could not climb up their stairs without being in pain. We helped to demonstrate the situation to our class, which in turn made it easier for the boy to understand and cope. We used a rectangle of paper and four blocks to "make a dog." The first dog had a long paper back with the block feet far apart to demonstrate the sagging painful back of the dachshund. We then demonstrated how a dog who was

	built differently did not get a sore back (legs closer together and back didn't sag). Our little friend felt so much happier that his pet was moving to a new house without steps and without pain.

TOY/SECURITY OBJECT: OUTGROWN	
Ideas to Explore	Sample Activities
• What happens to certain items when we get bigger (pacifiers, blankets, etc.)? • Strategies to use when we outgrow an object: ▸ Donate the object to someone who needs one. ▸ Replace it with something newer and more age appropriate. ▸ Pack the object away. ▸ Keep the item at home.	• Have a book or toy exchange. (Invite a group of children each to bring in a toy or book he or she no longer uses. Put them on display for all to see. Have each child choose a new toy or book to take home in its place.) • Collect and donate food, clothing, or toys to a shelter or other charity. • Cut a large blanket into a smaller hankie that can fit into an older child's pocket. • In order to retire old objects, pick "The Day" on a calendar. Cross off days on the calendar as "The Day" approaches or tear links off of a paper chain as you count down to the date. When the day arrives, put the pacifier in the "baby box," retire the old raggedy blanket for a new one, etc.

SUMMARY

Health encompasses an enormous amount of material. But it can be simplified quite nicely into a few different points:

- By teaching young children why sleep, nutrition, and exercise are important, by demonstrating stress reduction techniques with them and showing them how to cope with loss, by emphasizing the importance of preventative medical care, we intend for our children to be able to cope with the ups and downs of life in positive ways.

- Ask what your children know and what they want to know. First, clear up any misconceptions your children may have before you begin to answer their questions.

- Tell your children why something is good for their health and important to you.

- Be a good role model and take care of yourself. Because if you do not have good health or take proper care of yourself, you will be less able to care for your children. Plus, your children will be watching and learning from you.

CELEBRATING HEALTH THROUGHOUT THE YEAR

★

January:	Diet Resolution Week (First week)
	National Skating Month
	Oatmeal Month
	Shape Us Up Month
	International Year of Quinoa
	National Fresh Squeezed Juice Week (17-23)
	National Preschool Fitness Day (25)
	Meat Week (Last Sunday)
February:	National Nutrition Month
	National Sleep Awareness Month
	Children's Dental Health Month
	American Dental Association Give Kids a Smile Program (1)
	American Heart Month
	National Tooth Fairy Day (28)
March:	National Frozen Food Month
	National Nutrition Month
	National Sleep Awareness Week (First week)

National School Breakfast Week
(First week)

Act Happy Week (Third Monday)

Great American Meatout (20)

April: Stress Awareness Month

International Moment of Laughter (14)

National Stress Awareness Day (16)

World Tai Chi and Qigong Day (27)

Screen-Free Week Starts (End of April
through early May)

May: Mental Health Month

National Physical Fitness and
Sports Month

Healthy Vision Month

National Meditation Month

National Mental Health Month

National Physical Fitness and
Sports Month

National Salad Month

Garden Meditation Day (3)

Melanoma Monday (6)

World No Tobacco Day (31)

June:	National Fresh Fruits and Vegetables Month
	Child Vision Awareness Month
	Dairy Alternatives Month
	June Dairy Month
	Sports America Kids Month
	World Sauntering Day (19)
July:	Recreation and Parks Month
	National Make a Difference to Children Month
	Stay Out of the Sun Day (3)
August:	Children's Vision and Learning Month
	National Exercise with Your Child Week (First week)
	National Relaxation Day (15)
September:	National Five Servings of Fruits and Veggies a Day Month
	National Yoga Month
	International Self-Awareness Month
	National Skin Care Awareness Month
	Whole Grains Month
	International Clean Hands Week (Third week)

Family Health and Fitness Day (28)

October: National Audiology Awareness Month

World Vegetarian Day (1)

Walk to School Day (5)

Mental Illness Awareness Week
(First full week)

Child Health Day (7)

World Mental Health Day (10)

National School Lunch Week (Week
beginning the second Sunday)

November: Good Nutrition Month

World Immunization Month

Loosen Up, Lighten Up Day (14)

Great American Smokeout
(Third Thursday)

National Flossing Day (29)

December: National Hand-Washing Awareness
Week (First or second week)

World Peace Meditation (31)

Chapter Three

Communication

★

We have two ears and one mouth so that we can
listen twice as much as we speak.
– Epictetus

LESSONS IN COMMUNICATION

One of my favorite things to do with children is simply to
talk to them. Not just to share my version of wisdom with
them, but to learn about their views of the world. It is fas-
cinating, eye-opening, innocent, and often quite amusing.
And once I am able to see things from their perspective, I
can do a better job helping them to navigate their world.

Early in my career, I would visit day care centers and homes
that had special needs children enrolled in typical community programs. My job was to support the child, helping him
or her to have the same opportunities to grow and develop
as the other children in the classroom, while sharing the
goals that therapists recommended for the child's optimal
growth. Usually, I did this by supporting the teachers, who

typically did not plan to work with children with special needs. I helped the teachers to figure out how to meet the needs of the target child while meeting the needs of all of the other children in their care. I would observe the child in the classroom, providing suggestions on how he could more fully participate with his peers.

Sometimes, it was a matter of physically changing the setting. We might re-arrange the classroom, allowing for larger walkways, or hang curtains from the ceiling to provide smaller spaces and less distractions for the child. Sometimes, success was in reach by placing a sticky mat under a puzzle to hold it in place, or by putting a phonebook under a child's feet to help him sit in a chair without falling over so he could focus on eating. Sometimes, it entailed using simple sign language with a child who had language delays. At other times, we would break a task into smaller steps so a child could manage and learn a larger skill.

Here is what we did for four-year-old Austin, a sweet boy with Down Syndrome, who was learning to use the toilet. We broke the action of going potty into smaller steps, took photos of the steps, and taped the photos in the bathroom stall for Austin to read. "Pull down pants." "Sit on toilet." And so on. Well, one day, Austin's teacher added the words, "Turn around, Austin" to his procedure after he pulled his pants down. He proceeded to spin in circles, spraying everything in his path, including his surprised teacher! **Lesson #1: Children will take our words literally, some more than others.**

When I was a child care director in Germany, there was a four-year-old boy named Maxi who spoke very little, if any, English. In my beginner's German, I told him if he'd teach me German, then I would teach him English. We made a deal and shook hands. So each day, I'd stop in to see Maxi and he'd say "*Schmetterling*" and I'd reply with "butterfly," or I'd say "airplane" and he'd respond with "*Flugzeug.*" Mostly, he would giggle at my attempts to speak his native German.

After about a month, it was time for the Christmas holiday party. At school, we celebrated by having fruit punch and cookies. As I helped to serve the punch, Maxi approached me and asked, "*Ist das Gift?*" I assumed he was saying, "Is this a gift? Is this for me?" So I replied, "*Ya! Das ist fur dich.* This is for you." When Maxi just looked at me, I continued, "*Trinkst du. Das ist gut!* Drink it. It's good!" So Maxi drank his fruit punch and went on his way to play.

Later that evening, I excitedly told my husband that Maxi and I had an entire conversation instead of our usual word or two. He asked what our first real conversation was. When I relayed it to him, he said, "Karen, 'gift' in German means 'poison'." **Lesson #2: Our words can have a different meaning to the listener based on his or her experience and perspective. Remember to clarify and define things clearly for our little friends.**

A few years later when I was back teaching, I had my first experience in the United States with a non-English speaking child. Mauricio was from Madrid and did not know English, and none of us knew his native Spanish. I thought

I did a pretty good job explaining to the preschoolers that Mauricio spoke Spanish, so we were going to learn Spanish and he was going to learn English. The next morning, a perplexed and slightly frustrated four-year-old boy named Leo approached me upon arrival, exclaiming, "Karen, it didn't work! I tried it two times and it just didn't work!" I asked him what he was talking about. Leo said, "I went up to Mauricio and I said 'Spanish!' and nothing happened! So I said it again, and nothing happened! It doesn't work." **Lesson # 3: Providing examples of what to say is very important.**

I gathered the children together and said, "Leo taught me something important today. When I told you about Mauricio understanding Spanish and that we understand English, I didn't explain it very well. 'Spanish' is not a magic word we say and then we can understand each other. There is a Spanish word and a different English word for everything. For example, 'cat' in Spanish is '*gato*' and 'cat' in English is 'cat'." Once again, I was feeling pretty proud of my explanation and the children seemed to be learning some useful vocabulary. Then we jumped to the phrase, "Do you want to play with me?" The children all repeatedly asked Mauricio, "*Quieres jugar conmigo?*" and he excitedly said, "*Sí!*" The kids were so thrilled to say an entire sentence in Spanish, and to have Mauricio answer them in Spanish, that they repeated the phrase continuously to him, much to his confusion and dismay. Mauricio wanted to play and they just wanted to repeat "Do you want to play?" in Spanish! **Lesson #4: Teach useful words and phrases. Functional speech matters.**

I have learned a lot, thankfully, from the time I first worked with Austin, Maxi, and Mauricio. When YaYa, a native Chinese speaker, joined our classroom a year ago, I was much better prepared. I posted the pronunciations of Chinese words all around our classroom in the areas we were most likely to use those words (Examples: greetings on the door, colors in the art area, body parts and clothing in the bathroom, etc.). During Morning Meeting and informally throughout the day, my co-teacher, Jessica, and I would talk about tone of voice with the children, about how the sound of our voice conveys just as strong a message as our actual words do. We would act out scenarios using different tones of voice with different combinations of words and have the children interpret the situation. Nice words but harsh tone of voice? Kind tone of voice with nice words? Mad words with kind tone of voice?

We would add in facial expressions and have the children discuss and interpret those as well. A smile, a frown, a blank face, eye contact, or no eye contact all change the message received.

Next, gestures were added to the mix. A gentle tap on the shoulder to get a friend's attention or pointing to a toy or an area to play also change the dynamic.

Pretty soon, we would see our preschoolers asking YaYa "Do you want to play?" in English or Chinese, with an outstretched hand, a warm smile, and a gentle voice. YaYa learned to trust these kind souls, to take their hands, and allow herself to be led to the sensory table, the art table, or the dramatic play area. Kids would offer her their prized possessions, which she would accept. Soon, YaYa would make "chocolate" out of wood chips on the playground and offer them to anyone who would pass her "kitchen." Eventually, children would line up for one of her yummy treats. **Lesson #5: Sometimes the strongest form of communication is love and acceptance.**

EMPOWERING THE CHILDREN

What are some ways you can help your children become empowered communicators? Try some of these suggestions:

- Act out scenarios with your children to practice and prepare for real-life social situations. For example, asking someone to play or telling a friend you had a toy first. Use puppets, dolls, animals, cars, whatever your children like, or your own bodies as props.

    ‣ Use a different tone of voice with different combinations of words and have the children interpret the situation. Nice words but harsh tone of voice? Kind tone of voice with nice words? Mad words with kind tone of voice?

    ‣ Add in facial expressions and have children discuss and interpret those as well. A smile, a frown, a blank face, eye contact, or no eye contact all change the message received.

    ‣ Add gestures to the mix, such as a gentle tap on the shoulder to get a friend's attention or pointing to a toy or an area to play.

- Ask children whether they would want to play with a friend or sibling who talked to them or treated them unkindly. Why or why not? What could they do differently to make them want to play together?

HOW DO YOU TALK ABOUT THE LAND OF THE ALLIGATORS?

My daughter Michaele just graduated in May from Tulane. Over the four years she was living in New Orleans, my husband John and I made quite a few trips down south to enjoy the food, music, and culture that is uniquely New Orleans.

As a teacher, I was always on the lookout for things to share with the kids in my Pre-K classroom. We would dance to Cajun music and try to figure out what some of the Cajun words were when we sat down for a break. We would look at books written and illustrated by George Rodrigue, who first began drawing *Blue Dog* when he was five years old. And I would tell stories about delicious alligator cheesecake that is a specialty at Jacques Imos Restaurant.

Of course, stories about alligators are never enough when you can have real alligators brought into the classroom. I would bring alligator jerky for the children to try during our weekly "Eat the Alphabet" program. They would try plain alligator, Cajun alligator, and barbecue alligator. And no matter how much I brought to school, there was never enough alligator to eat, especially the Cajun spice flavor for these adventurous, young Seattle-ites!

Last fall during a trip to see my daughter, I decided I must have an alligator head to bring back to the classroom. I knew the kids would love it, and the alligator would have a place of honor in our science area. Little did I know that purchasing this alligator head would result in deep discussions and difficult questions about animal rights. And little did I know that I would have the chance to buy my alligator head directly from the front seat of the taxicab that took us from the airport to our hotel that first night!

The taxi driver was a large man who sounded a bit like Fats Domino when he spoke. He proceeded to tell us, to the surprise of my jet-lagged husband, everything you ever wanted to know about alligators. He told us that four-foot alligators make the best sandwiches if you "just put the tail between two pieces of bread!", that there is a great alligator farm we could visit for a tour, and that there are over 100 ways to prepare alligator. And so on. It was a great moment for me, and for the taxi driver. I collected plenty of material to share with my class and he was $20 richer.

When I returned to Seattle, the kids were very excited to see what I brought back with me. Everyone had lots of questions, and it was my job to answer them to the best of my ability:

Was it a real alligator, for real life? ("For real life" is the ultimate way to differentiate between real and pretend for little kids.) Yes. But the eyes are marbles.

Why are the eyes marbles? You know how apples get brown, mushy, and start to get rotten after no one eats them? The same thing would happen to the eyes if the real eyes were in the alligator. And they would get stinky.

Why would they get stinky? Since the alligator is not alive anymore, germs would get on the eyes and the germs would use them for food. They would rot away and begin to smell.

Are the teeth real, for real life? Yes, the teeth are real. But the alligator can't bite you because he isn't alive anymore. You can safely touch the teeth because what's our #1 rule? *SAFETY FIRST!*

Why did you only bring back the head of the alligator? The people who raised the alligator used the rest of the alligator for food and other things. In fact, the taxi driver told me that this alligator was four feet long, and that is the perfect size for making the best alligator sandwich you've ever eaten in your life! Also, people use the alligator skin for belts, wallets, and shoes, and make jewelry from the teeth. (I also showed them the brochure and video clip from the alligator farm.)

Why do people eat alligators? Because there are lots of alligators in New Orleans. We eat lots of fish and salmon because we have lots of fish in Seattle. Other places may eat more chicken or venison because there are more of those animals living there.

Why do people hate alligators and chop their heads off? (I am possibly getting into dangerous territory here!) They don't hate them. In fact, the people at the alligator farm really love the alligators and take good care of them. They feed them healthy food and give the alligators a comfortable place to live. People can go on tours to see how the alligators are treated while they are alive. When it is time to kill the alligators, the people at the alligator farm try to kill them as respectfully as possible so the alligators do not suffer needlessly.

How do they chop off their heads? (YIKES! I feel like I need to address this now or it could turn into a crazier or more confusing situation. Plus, the kids are *so* interested and on the edge of their seats!) Well, I haven't seen it done, but I would guess they would use a very sharp knife so they only have to cut once. How does it feel to you when someone pulls off a Band-Aid really slowly and takes a long time? It hurts, right? But if you do it one time quickly, it doesn't hurt as much. I'm sure the people who have to kill the alligators try to do it quickly so the alligators don't hurt as much. I would also think the people who work at the alligator farm feel it in their hearts when they have to do this job. And maybe they feel a little better knowing they will not waste the alligator. That they will use the alligator for food and use the rest of the animal for shoes, belts, and teaching kids about alligators, letting them touch the alligators without getting bitten by sharp teeth. If I worked there, I know I would thank the alligators for providing me with so many things. (Again, YIKES! Just so you know, if I had it to do over, I would tell the kids I needed to research how the people kill the alligators and I would get back to them. I would also say that the people probably did not cut their heads off while the alligators were still alive. Chalk that up to a lesson learned!)

This conversation went on for forty-five minutes. I believe most of the kids went home with many stories that evening.

The next day, Julia, one of my little students who has an enormous capacity for detail, and her mom came in bright and early. Her mom said, "Julia talked all night about all the things you can make from an alligator and all the ways you can eat an alligator. She sounded like Bubba from *Forrest Gump*! The story sounded so crazy, I knew it had to be true!"

Three-year-old Elise was also telling her parents about it. When they asked where Michaele went to college, she replied, "I think it is called *The Land of the Alligators.*" A few months later, friends of Elise's family had the sad occurrence of their family dog dying. One of the first questions from Elise's mouth was, "Did they cut off its head so they could give it to a teacher and kids could learn about dog heads?"

A year later, I was talking to another parent. Maya's mom reflected, "I was originally a little fearful about what would come from the alligator conversation. Maya still remembers it clearly and talks about it. But she has made the focus more about animal rights. Why do people eat animals? Is this the right thing to do? Sometimes, she does not want to eat fish and that is okay."

Yes, it is okay.

EMPOWERING THE CHILDREN

Communicating with other people is a skill we will use our entire lives. To help your children become successful communicators, here are some ideas:

- Teach children to "Stop, look, and listen." This means stop your activity, make eye contact with the speaker, and listen to his words before acting. Practice it in different situations (small or large groups, quiet or noisy settings).

- Teach children how to ask questions, beginning with getting someone's attention. Depending on the situation, it may be learning to say, "Excuse me," raising a hand to be called on, or tapping someone on the shoulder. Practice it!

- Teach children how to find answers besides asking an adult. Don't be afraid to say, "I don't know." Then show your child how you would find an answer. This process demonstrates how to be a capable problem-solver without having to know all the answers or being afraid to make a mistake.

    ▸ Ask a friend.

    ▸ Look in a book or on a computer.

    ▸ Think it over for a while before making your decision.

    ▸ Do an experiment.

- Demonstrate and practice admitting mistakes and how to make amends.

- Read the book *Communication* by Aliki. This book does a great job of explaining the different ways people communicate verbally and nonverbally, with skills varying based on a person's age and practice. It addresses the forms of communication (conversations in person, written, over the phone, etc.) and how to communicate in different situations. The book also stresses the importance of communication and makes the point that poor communication can lead to misunderstandings, even war between countries.

▸ My co-teacher and I thought this book was so valuable that we sent it home with each child for a few nights. We wanted them to share it with their parents.

▸ A few weeks passed. One afternoon, I heard two friends arguing in the area of our classroom that contains wooden blocks and animals. As I approached, little Julia, who was barely four at the time, actually got to the arguing kids first and placed a hand on each one's shoulder. She looked in their eyes and said, "Do you really want to start a war?" They stopped arguing, exclaimed "No!" and hugged each other before returning to play. That was a proud and joyful moment for me!

BULLYING BEHAVIORS

Good communication skills set the foundation for getting along with other people. When our communication skills are not well-developed, fighting can occur easily. But what is the difference between a simple disagreement and bullying behavior, which has received a lot of press for the past few years? Let's look at bullying the same way we would look at a topic with our children, by first clearing up any misconceptions we may have about it. I will give you some practical suggestions to use with the children in your family or your classroom, but first a little discussion on fighting.

We've all heard the message of telling children to hit back if someone hits them. If you are attacked by a bully, fight back. As a child, I was afraid that if someone physically attacked me and I retaliated, then I would be injured and I would be labeled a fighter, which has its own set of consequences. Even at an early age, I was aware that when someone hit another child back, the fight would escalate and one if not both of the children would end up physically injured and always angrier. This option has never felt right or made sense to me, and now the research is showing my instincts were correct. (More about how to handle this situation in the Empowering the Children section below.)

What exactly are we talking about when we use the term "bullying?" When our children take toys from a peer, hit their brother, or call someone a name, does this behavior mean the child is a bully? Not necessarily. All children refine their social and emotional skills as they grow up and need time to practice what they have learned. So not all aggressive behaviors are considered bullying.

What makes bullying unique is the intention and the frequency of the aggression. To be a bully, a person's intentional behavior must be done repeatedly and from a position of real or perceived power. To elaborate, real power may take the form of physical size or age, while perceived power may come from popularity, knowing some secret we intend to use against another person, or differences in wealth, skin color, language, and the list goes on.

There are three types of bullying:

- Verbal: This form presents itself as name-calling, teasing, and/or threatening another person with spoken or written words.

- Social: This form is more common in girls and is recognized as leaving someone out on purpose, telling other children not to be friends with someone, spreading rumors about someone, and embarrassing someone in public. The goal here is to harm a peer's relationships or reputation.

- Physical: This form is more common in boys and involves hurting a person's body or possessions by physical actions such as hitting, kicking, pinching, spitting, tripping, pushing someone, or taking or breaking someone's belongings.

If left unchecked, harassment behaviors may turn into full-blown bullying. In these cases, adults must intervene and teach children how to handle conflict appropriately. According to researcher J.M. Ostrov[1], about 20 percent of high school and nearly 30 percent of middle school students experience bullying at some point. Luckily, preschool bullying usually occurs right in front of parents and teachers, allowing us the opportunity to act immediately. It is a bit trickier with older children who may act one way in front of adults and another when unsupervised.

Ironically, preschoolers who are bullied often become the bullies years later, and conversely, bullies often become the bullied. Why is this? Peers isolate the bullies because of their aggression, do not want to play with them, and exclude them from social activities. Bullied children learn to retaliate in the same way they were treated as preschoolers

---

1 Ostrov, J. M. "Forms of aggression and peer victimization during early childhood: A short-term longitudinal study." *Journal of Abnormal Child Psychology*. 36 (2008): 311-322.

and become the new bullies. Both kids who are bullied and who bully others may develop long-term problems. Adults must intervene to stop this vicious cycle from spinning out of control and damaging our children. Of course, bullying can begin at any age, not just during preschool.

A great starting point is to examine how we feel about the word "conflict." Most people immediately think of a frustrating situation, something they want to avoid. It is actually more productive to view conflict as an opportunity to learn and grow since that makes it much easier for us to be prepared for and feel capable of handling conflicts. As Linda Lantieri and Janet Patti state in *Waging Peace in Our Schools,* conflict is a problem to be solved, not a contest to be won. By modeling and teaching pro-social behaviors, most conflicts can be solved peacefully.

ACTIVITY: REASSESSING CONFLICT

- How do you feel when you hear the word "conflict"?
  - ▸ Pay attention to your breathing, the feeling in your chest, your muscles.
  - ▸ What conflicts stress you out?
- Now think about one of those situations in a new light.
  - ▸ Breathe in and out deeply.
  - ▸ Think of this as an opportunity to learn and grow.
  - ▸ What solutions come to mind?
  - ▸ How do you feel?

Certainly, we need to demonstrate appropriate and desired behavior in front of our kids. Besides leading by example, what else can be done to teach a child how to act? Not only do we consciously have to be a good role model for our children, but we also have to tell our children what to say and what to do in order to solve conflicts when they do not know how to proceed. Most importantly, we then need to *practice the words and actions with kids in order for them to develop this skill and make it their own.* By instructing our children to tell the aggressor calmly how his actions are affecting them and that it is not acceptable to treat them in this way, the bully learns that his actions are not rewarded. Example: "It hurts my arm when you pinch me. I don't like that. I don't like to play with people who hurt my body or my feelings."

When I was teaching with Jessica, we would take advantage of those teachable moments *when something was occurring* to instruct the child and have him practice it then and there with his aggressor. At other times, we would practice scenarios or situations as part of a group meeting, using animals, puppets, or simply ourselves as "props" to act out the situation first. We would try multiple scenarios, some that worked and some that didn't, in front of the children, having them critique us on what worked, what didn't, and why. Then they tried it with a teacher in front of the group or with another peer.

William Kriedler, author of *The Peaceable Classroom*, states, "When people respond to anger assertively and say what they feel in a way that other people can hear, they are acting strongly, because they have put themselves in a position where they can best change what it is that's angering them." Not only is it strong to use our voices instead of our fists to make our point, but we need to use a strong, confident voice while making our point. An assertive voice is not an aggressive voice, nor a meek voice. We need to practice this strong voice with our children as well.

When we find our children behaving inappropriately, it is the loving and moral thing to do to call them on their behavior, show them how to do better, and lead by example, whether we are parents, teachers, or friends. In fact, research reinforces the effectiveness of stepping in. When we ignore bullying behaviors, they increase. When those in authority make it clear that bullying will not be tolerated, the behaviors decrease or cease to exist.

Perhaps it is easy to understand that physical aggression is never to be tolerated. But we may be less educated on how children learn racial prejudice and what differences children observe on their own at certain ages. The following developmental milestones reflect the ages at which children become aware of certain differences:

- Age 2: children notice differences in gender and skin color.

- Age 3: children notice societal norms based upon gender, racial differences, and physical abilities.

- Ages 3-5: children describe themselves based on skin color, gender, and abilities.

- Ages 4-5: children make biased comments based on race, gender, and physical attributes.

Obviously, we all want the same end result: children who feel capable and confident, treat others with respect, value the differences we all bring to the table, and can contribute in a positive manner at home, school, and work. *However, if even one individual child doesn't feel safe in a setting, then none of the children in the group can truly feel safe.* In my years of experience, I have observed children become more worried, agitated, or stressed when another child "gets away with" bullying. I think this stress results from the child possibly feeling like a potential future victim, and thus, he or she is on edge. It is our job as caring and responsible parents and teachers to make sure all children feel safe in our care.

EMPOWERING THE CHILDREN

What are some concrete activities we can do with our children to help them along the way toward peaceful interactions with others?

- To prevent prejudice, acknowledge that while every person is special, everyone is also a member of a group. Every group, even our own, has both positive and negative qualities to it.

- Schools need to be crystal clear that their message is strong against violence and bias (including the curriculum, bulletin boards, school activities, discipline procedures) and have strong sanctions in place against transgressions. This uniformity in the message is the only path of ensuring emotional and physical safety for children.

- Have a "no exclusion" policy of participation, meaning we must not exclude someone because of who he or she is. However, it is an appropriate sanction to say, "I don't want to play with you because you ripped my drawing (or hit me, called me a name, etc.)." This policy applies at home and at school.

- Encourage cooperation by putting diverse groups together to work toward a common goal. For little guys, it could simply be finding all of the red items in the room and collecting them in a box, sharing the easel for partner art, or carrying a large item across the room or playground together.

- Enact a "Safety first" rule that relates to bodies, ideas, feelings, work, and possessions. For example, "We will not play (read, go outside, cross the street, etc.) until you are sitting safely in your chair (are holding hands with your partner, put the stick on the ground, are listening to my words, check to see whether Anna is hurt, etc.)."

- Teach children how to consider more than one point of view. Show different perspectives in the same story by reading different versions of a familiar tale, such as *The Three Little Pigs*. Discuss and change sides when role-playing a scenario to see what the other side feels like. Act out different characters in a play.

- Compare and contrast similar items (colors, vehicles, books, shells, etc.). Do you like one more than the others? Why?

- Sort toys by more than one attribute. Example: Sort toy cats by color, then by tails up or down, sitting or standing, or wanting to eat a fish or a mouse. Lesson learned: People are defined by more than one aspect of themselves.

- Explore games of cause and effect by making logical connections between events, which can be related to real life situations. ("Remember how the ball knocked the bowling pin over? That's what happened when you ran into Jim; you knocked him down. Let's help him up and check on his body.")

- Have the aggressor imagine he is draining all of his negative feelings out of his body, so they are collecting into a puddle on the floor. Wipe them up and dispose of them in the garbage can.

- At home and school, have a Peace Corner (filled with relaxation items) or Peace Table (a safe and neutral spot to talk about a problem with respect, listen to each other, and decide how to solve the problem). Tools like these help children learn that they have power because they can make choices, and they are responsible for what they say and what they do. Over time, kids will internalize the skills required for solving conflicts with others or relaxing their overly stressed bodies. They will be able to use their internalized skills even when a Peace Table or Peace Corner is not available.

- Provide activities that help children develop healthy identities such as looking in mirrors, drawing self-portraits, and playing "Who am I?" (Help them identify each other with photos of their hands, the back of their heads, their feet, etc.)

- It is also important to teach the positive and negative associations with colors and characters of color.

▸ For example, the color blue is associated with calm, cold, and feeling sad.

▸ Be sure to use the colors brown and black as beautiful decorations and not refer to them as "ugly" colors.

▸ Represent heroes in the classroom or home (dolls, books, posters, etc.) with people or characters from the same cultural background as your children as well as those from the cultures of the "friends we have not met yet." This process also helps to ease the fears many children have when joining a new school, beginning a new activity like dance class, or even playing at the park where they may not know anyone else. Strangers can be considered as potential new friends instead of people to be feared.

• Discuss how grumpy or uncooperative behavior affects everyone in the home or classroom. Just like laughter, it is contagious.

One last point must be added: peace education needs to be part of our entire curriculum, from little kids on up. It cannot be just an extra thirty minutes added to the activities of the week; it must be blended into the activities of the moment in order to be successful. A bit more effort in the beginning will lead to a more smoothly running classroom and home environment in the long run.

Children who enjoy peaceable classrooms have experienced the power of constructive action, and they are more hopeful about tackling problems and effecting social change. They see what the larger world can be like and are happy to be a part in making it a reality. Paraphrasing Holocaust survivor Jacob Riis, as he uses the image of a stonecutter, "Whether our act of interrupting prejudice is the first or the last before a change occurs in a person, our job is to keep hammering the stone until it breaks."

SUMMARY

Communicating with others is one of the most important things we do as humans. It is one of the building blocks of the foundation of a successful human being that must be taught to children. Although language is natural for us, communicating effectively is a bit of an art.

- Look at your own words, the intentions behind your message, as well as how you and other adults deliver your messages to children.

- Don't be afraid if you don't know an answer. Acknowledge your children's questions, tell them you'll find an answer or make a decision, and always follow-through with what you say you will do.

- Respond immediately to inappropriate behaviors such as bullying.

- Remember how much can be learned by listening to each other.

CELEBRATING COMMUNICATION
THROUGHOUT THE YEAR

★

January: National Hug Day (21)

Belly Laugh Day (24)

February: Take Your Child to the Library Day (2)

Children's Authors and Illustrators
Week (First full week)

Wave All Your Fingers at Your
Neighbors Day (7)

Valentine's Day (14)

International Mother Language
Day (21)

March: Colic Awareness Month

Deaf History Month

International Listening Awareness
Month

National Write a Letter of
Appreciation Month

Optimism Month

Sing with Your Child Month

World Compliment Day (1)

International Tongue Twister
Contest (2)

NEA's Read Across America Day (2)

Make Up Your Own Holiday Day (26)

April: National Card & Letter Writing Month

National Humor Month

School Library Month

Reading is Fun Day (1)

International Children's Book Day (2)

National Siblings Day (10)

National Library Week (mid-month)

May: Better Hearing and Speech Month

Global Civility Month

National Photo Month

Great American Grump Out (1)

Hug Your Cat Day (3)

National Stuttering Awareness Week (Second week)

June: Effective Communications Month

July: National Make a Difference to Children Month

National Tell an Old Joke Day (24)

August: National Tell a Joke Day (16)

September: International People Skills Month

International Enthusiasm Week (1-7)

Love Note Day (27)

R.E.A.D. in America Day (28)

October: Celebrating the Bilingual Child Month

Emotional Intelligence Month

National Bullying Prevention Month

World Smile Day (3)

International Stuttering Awareness Day (22)

November: Picture Book Month

National Family Literacy Day (1)

I Love to Write Day (15)

World Hello Day (21)

Better Conversation Week (Thanksgiving week)

National Day of Listening (29)

December: Letter Writing Day (7)

Chapter Four

Problem-Solving

★

There are three ways you can get to the top of a
tree: I) sit on an acorn 2) make friends with
a bird 3) climb it.
– Anonymous

As a teacher of young children, I have always enjoyed getting them involved in solving their own problems, whether
the problem is a disagreement over a toy, a reluctance to
follow a rule, or the discovery that there are bigger issues
than ourselves in the world. In this chapter, I will share a
few examples of children discovering their power to solve
problems and what to do if something isn't working.

MAKING A DIFFERENCE, ONE BABY TOOTH AT A TIME

"Karen! I have something *so* important to tell you! Did you
know that some kids don't get to go to the dentist when they
are little? And their teeth hurt them! What can we do to
help?" My little friend Zoe was out of breath and had a very

worried look on her face. She was handing me the newspaper article that she had carefully cut out of the paper that morning ("Kids' teeth crusader leads new care center," *Seattle Times*, August 19, 2010).

Even though she was just over four years old at the time, Zoe had already developed the habit of exploring the newspaper before school. The children, my co-teacher, and I would bring in anything of interest to put in our "Magic Suitcase" for Morning Meeting. Morning Meeting was our version of Circle Time, our daily opportunity to learn about the calendar and the weather, read stories, play games, and discuss our curriculum as a group. During this time, we would pull out the articles and talk about issues that interested or concerned our classroom community. Usually, the topics would involve animals, weather, or natural disasters. Sometimes, we would hang up the stories or pictures on the wall or add them to one of our homemade books (*Animals in the News,* for example). At other times, we would build our curriculum off the topic if the children were very interested in the subject matter. That is exactly what happened in this situation.

I actually had read the same story that very morning and already placed a copy in the Magic Suitcase. But I happily replaced my copy with Zoe's. This was one of the first times I had seen Zoe so passionate about a topic. Because she loved being the "Weather Girl" during our meeting time, she usually looked at the forecast to help prepare herself for predicting what clothing we'd need for outdoor time. But today was different.

Zoe was attracted to a photo of a cute three-month-old baby named Harrison who was getting his first dental exam at the brand new Center for Pediatric Dentistry. Zoe's mother Liz explained that even babies need to get their teeth and gums checked by the dentist. Liz went on to explain that the reporter wrote the article because in the state of Washington, almost half of the children under age five never visited a dentist, that 60 percent of elementary school children had tooth decay, and 20 percent of those children had decay in seven or more teeth. With her mom's help, Zoe realized that this was a serious situation, and a painful situation, for people like herself.

"What should we do? Should we buy lots of those little toothpastes and give them to all the kids?" Zoe wanted to know. I encouraged her to explain the situation to her friends at Morning Meeting so we could come up with a plan. She was so inspired by this article that she could barely wait for the other children to arrive so we could begin our discussion.

At Morning Meeting, Zoe came to the front of the group. "Guys, this is serious." She told the other children about the article, we looked at the picture of Baby Harrison, and we wrote down what we knew:

- Harrison went to the dentist, even though he didn't have any teeth. How did his mom and dad know to take him? Some of us had never been to the dentist before and all of us had teeth!

- There was a brand new Center for Pediatric Dentistry. There were people who worked there who knew how to help kids with teeth problems.

- We wanted to help too!

NEXT, WE CAME UP WITH OUR PLAN FOR EMPOWERMENT:

- We called the Center for Pediatric Dentistry to see how we could help spread the important word about going to the dentist. After talking to the outreach worker, we decided to design our own flier to hang around our school, deliver to other classrooms, and provide to local pediatricians for their offices. The Trailblazers (my kids' group name) also talked to the other students and teachers in our school to help pass on what they knew about going to the dentist and brushing their teeth.

- The staff at the Center for Pediatric Dentistry used their special connections to arrange for the Tooth Fairy to visit our classroom! (Although I have no proof, I believe the Tooth Fairy was actually an intern at the Center for Pediatric Dentistry.) The Tooth Fairy helped to explain the finer details of her job ("I can fly as fast as Fairy Speed Eleven. But most of the time, I only need to fly at Fairy Speed Seven in order to collect all the teeth each night.") as well as let us brush her stuffed lion's teeth with the biggest toothbrush you've ever seen. Before she left, she gave the children their own goodie bags, each with a toothbrush, toothpaste, and dental floss. Very cool!

- We invited Baby Harrison and his parents to visit our classroom so we could thank them for being in the newspaper. We wanted to tell them everything we learned about how important dental health is for everyone, even kids without teeth. In preparation for the family's visit, Zoe and her friends made homemade toys for Harrison (shakers and bottles with decorative items floating in them for him to observe)!

- We invited a classroom parent who is also a dentist to visit our classroom. Manav's mom, Ritu, brought her bag of tools, letting us try out the special dental glasses, mirrors, and plastic flossing picks, allowing us to pretend to be actual dentists for the morning.

- We took a field trip to see the Center for Pediatric Dentistry with our own eyes. For some of the children, it was their first time to sit in a dentist's chair. They were now confident and excited to have their parents take them for their very own dentist visits!

- A few other lessons we did in relation to dental care included:

  ▶ Feeding dolls "food" and then brushing their teeth.

  ▶ Brushing ferocious dinosaurs' teeth.

  ▶ Painting plastic skulls and teeth green, and then brushing the teeth white again.

  ▶ Making homemade toothpaste.

  ▶ Eating healthy foods.

  ▶ Looking at our teeth in hand mirrors.

  ▶ Wearing vampire teeth.

▸ Observing the effect of vinegar on a raw egg (in the shell), since it eats through the eggshell just like acid eats through the enamel on teeth.

We learned a variety of useful facts and answered many of our questions thanks to that newspaper article. However, I think the most important lessons were the ones learned by Zoe on that day she arrived at school with such passion and concern for the other children in the world. Zoe learned that she did not have to wait to be a grown-up to make a difference. She learned that she could find an issue that was important to her and try to find her own way to address the problem today.

As a teacher and a parent, I wondered what Zoe would remember about these experiences today, two years later. I recently spent a couple of hours with Zoe and her mom to find out.

Zoe, a bright girl with warm hazel-brown eyes, is now in first grade. She exudes confidence as she tells stories about her adventures in life, and more than once spontaneously exclaimed, "I'm gonna do this!" as she elaborated on her efforts to try to fly (Yes, by flapping her arms!) and climbing ropes.

When I asked Zoe about her memories related to the newspaper article, she smiled as she explained how the Tooth Fairy, whom she was able to see *twice*, has magic that only allows her to fly at night when kids are sleeping. She reported enjoying visiting the dentist now, rewards of tattoos and toys being very motivating, but recalled crying when very little because she personally didn't understand why the dentist was putting his hand in her mouth. Zoe said it makes her excited and happy to think about helping other kids, and her mom remembers how proud Zoe was at the time to be the spark to the events happening in our classroom. Another high point? Brushing the green skeleton teeth so they would be bright and white again!

Our four-year-old who loved to check the newspaper everyday still does so at age six, first to see whether it is warm enough for shorts, and second to search for interesting pictures, words, and numbers. And Zoe and her mom Liz are still looking for ways to help others in the community. Their current project—volunteering at the neighborhood food bank.

If Zoe could give one bit of advice to other kids, it would be: "Just learn how to do things you haven't learned. Jump rope, do math, run. It's all important." I think this advice is good for people of all ages. Thanks for teaching us, Zoe!

There's no use talking about the problem unless you talk about the solution.
– Betty Williams

THE MELTING GLACIERS: KIDS WANT TO HELP MAKE A DIFFERENCE

Danny Westneat, a *Seattle Times* staff columnist, recently wrote about his summer trip to Glacier National Park ("No more glaciers? Imagine that," August 14, 2012). He was distressed to find out from the park rangers that the glaciers are melting much more quickly than predicted, and they may disappear completely by 2020. His children were expecting to slide in the snow like their father did as a child, but they only caught glimpses of white in the remote distance. Because of the effects of climate change and human-produced global warming, Westneat said it is too late to save the glaciers, so tourists may as well drive over to Glacier National Park to see the glaciers before they are gone.

Two weeks later, Westneat wrote "A Win In the War On Warming"(August 29, 2012) in response to the letters he received from his original article. Some people were upset that he wrote about the disappearing glaciers without mentioning any possible solutions to the problem. In his own defense, Mr. Westneat wrote, "The researchers who study the park told me these glaciers are cooked. The warming today is due in part to fossil fuels burned years ago." Although the Obama Administration and the auto industry are finally working together and have agreed to "nearly double the fuel efficiency of U.S. cars and trucks by 2025, to an average of 54.5 mpg across the entire fleet," Westneat was attending to his job of writing about the current state of things, not proposing huge policy solutions. "That's what national leaders are supposed to be for," Westneat said.

Danny Westneat is correct; it is the job of our policy makers to propose policy solutions. But it seems that politicians in general have gotten bogged down in partisan issues and often have trouble moving forward, or even have difficulty generating new ideas. I thought it might be interesting to visit a few of my colleagues and their groups of preschoolers to find out what the children's thoughts were on this issue.

Before heading to Hutch Kids Child Care Center, I did a little of my own research first. Even though the children are just three and four years old, it is still important to have the facts correct and anticipate a few of their questions. Since we reside in Seattle, which is in the Pacific Northwest and relatively close to Glacier National Park, I wanted to be able to express how the changes at the park might affect the children who live in this area, as well as what they can do as individuals or as a group to make an impact on the local community and larger world[1]. I decided to break the topic into smaller segments, for ease of understanding and simplifying the issues.

Since I was only visiting the classrooms for a few hours, I brought this information with me and left it with the children's teachers in case they had questions later in the day, week, or month. This extra information is included here to provide an example of the types of questions teachers and parents can be prepared for and examples of simple factual answers to give to young children. Again, as the adult who knows your children best, you would pick and choose what to discuss based on their questions, depth of understanding, and interest in the topic.

WHAT IS THE PROBLEM?

Simply put, snow and ice melt faster than new snow can come down due to warmer winter temperatures and less precipitation in the form of snow and rain. As teacher Jessica Higinbotham further elaborated to her class, "It is

---

1 Visit www.epa.gov/climatechange/impacts-adaptation/northwest.html for my source for the information I shared with my students.

like your freezer is broken and now it can't keep your ice cream cold enough. It just keeps melting."

WHY DOES IT MATTER?

Melting glaciers add more water to the oceans, causing beaches to disappear and cities to flood, which in turn causes people to lose their homes and businesses. Wetlands, which usually buffer communities from flood waters and are home to many plants and animals, are destroyed. And the storms keep coming because warmer weather generates more storms. Warmer temperatures cause decreasing snow in the mountains, meaning there is less water in the streams, producing more competition for water among people, animals, and plants.

Since much of the region's water is stored naturally in the mountainous winter snowpack, it's predicted that the Cascades may suffer a 40 percent decrease in its winter snowpack by the 2040s. Warmer weather also causes more precipitation to fall as rain, which decreases snow accumulation and increases the risk of winter floods. Logically, less water in the summer streams increases the risk of summer drought, which will reduce hydroelectricity. This situation is serious since 70 percent of our electricity here in the Northwest is hydroelectricity. What electricity we produce will also be further burdened since rising temperatures will increase the demand for air conditioning and refrigeration.

Drier conditions create another unsavory side effect—an increase in the presence of pests and disease in our trees and food sources, threatening the survival of our forests and agriculture. It naturally follows that a higher risk of forest fires and a decrease in tree growth can change the composition, range, and even existence of the Northwest tree species. The apple trees in the Northwest are at particular risk, as are other fruit-bearing trees.

WHAT CAN PEOPLE DO ABOUT IT?

- Protect or restore the wetlands and beaches.

- Improve the storm drainage systems in our communities.

- Build protective barriers where necessary.

- Switch to clean energy such as solar and wind power.

- Use less energy overall by doing simple things like turning off the TV and lights when they are not in use.

- Travel green by walking, biking, or using public transportation when possible.

- Limit water use by turning off the water when brushing teeth.

- Plant more native drought-resistant plants in yards.

- Reduce waste by bringing your own reusable bag to the store rather than using plastic or paper bags that are bad for the environment.

- Recycle, compost, and reuse items.

- Plant a tree to provide the environment with more oxygen, produce shade, prevent erosion, and provide habitat for birds or other creatures.

- Buy locally grown food, plant a garden, and visit farmers markets.

- Spread the word, teaching adults and kids alike the different ways they can make a difference. By working together, one small act by one person is transformed into many acts, making a large impact!

VISITING THE CLASSROOMS

My former co-teacher Jessica and teacher Sam Garcia had gathered the three- and four-year-old children together in the Moons and Stars classroom for my visit. After briefly discussing the newspaper articles from Danny Westneat, looking at photos from Glacier National Park, and both identifying animals that might live there and activities people might do while visiting, the children were very pleased to realize that they could help save glaciers. As they squealed, "I can! How?" I immediately told them I was interested in hearing what ideas they had about saving the glaciers, protecting the earth, or helping in the future. Here are some of their responses:

- Beck solemnly shared, "I think the glaciers will die and we won't be able to play with them. I like to walk on them."

- Maddie, who had visited Glacier National Park the previous week, had a lot to tell us. She reminded us, "We need enough water for people; for all people. They have a big red bus (at Glacier); I rode in it and didn't ride in my car. And we can ride bicycles."

- Chiyo had the novel idea "If there's snow coming down in the winter, then we need a snow globe. Put it all in the snow globe to save it. And we can walk; don't drive every day."

- That prompted Sahana, who eagerly exclaimed, "You can put the glaciers in a net. And drive on the bus!" She also remembered, "We turn off the light when we go to the playground."

- Cora, proud of the fact that she and her whole family do something every day to help be "gentle to the Earth," said, "We have a park right next to my house and I can just walk right to it!"

EMPOWERING THE CHILDREN

Then we moved our discussion to the table, where we had sensory tubs filled with icebergs (large, medium, and smaller cubes of ice), polar animals, whales, water, eye droppers, and cups of warm water. Here is what the children learned from our discussion:

- As Chiyo was holding her finger on the block of ice, slowly melting a hole through it, she commented, "It takes a long, long time. But why don't animals melt?" Opportunity: Discuss and experiment to show how it usually takes a long time for big pieces of ice to melt and less time for smaller pieces to melt. Relate this information to the glaciers at Glacier National Park, the polar ice caps, etc. Discuss the different properties of water vs. solid materials such as bones, muscles, and fur. Can they freeze? Can they melt?

- Sam took advantage of a teachable moment as the ice melted by asking the kids to consider "Do you notice something about the water?" Sahana and Jack answered, "It's getting deeper." Opportunity: You can take this further and come up with potential problems of too much melting water coming down the mountain at once. What might happen? What could you do to help?

- While Jack was exploring the polar bears and ice, he noticed and exclaimed, "It's (ice) getting smaller! The polar bear will fall! In the voice of a worried bear, he squealed, "I'm slipping! I'm falling! I might die!" Opportunity: Ask why the bear might die. What would need to happen to the water to make it return to the form of ice in nature and in the classroom?

- To Cora's surprise, as she spoke for her seal, asking to be saved from the melting ice shelf, Sahana's bear announced, "Jump on my back! I'll save you!" Opportunity: Discuss why the bear would help the seal. Is it because the animals are friends? The bear and the seal are different kinds of animals; can two different kinds of animals be friends? Can two different kinds of people be friends and help each other? Why or why not?

- Louie, pouring water over his ice, said, "It cracked! It breaked! Oh no!" Opportunity: Discuss how and why water breaks ice. What happens after it cracks or breaks?

I also visited the Rainforest classroom, which has a majority of four year olds enrolled. Teachers Julie Holmes and Ryan Bunda participated in a similar discussion. The children made many comments and observations:

- When discussing topics of alternatives to driving cars, Ben suggested "driving a bus or the monorail." Seattle is fortunate to have a one-mile track for our monorail train above our city streets to cut down on car traffic in our downtown area.

- Kaida was quick to point out, "We can walk and it keeps us exercised."

- After her initial surprise ("I didn't know we could save the earth!"), Maya had a thought: "We could take everything out (of the mountains) and wait 'til all the snow melts. Then start over."

Clearly, these young people were able to grasp the seriousness of the situation and were eager to try to think of ways to help. A few things they came up with included: turning off the TV (Maya), "use things from the recycle bin and then use them again" (Henry), and "turning out the lights" (Tilia and Gregory).

EMPOWERING THE CHILDREN

When this group moved to the table for iceberg and animal play, they also made some discoveries:

- When Kaida noticed Maya's ice melting quickly, Maya shared her technique: "I put my hands on it for a long time." Maxine commented, "The ice makes my hands wet because it's melting. I can make it melt very fast; I'm rubbing it and then I let it sit." Ivy replied, "When the ice melts, it gets smaller. If the ice and the snow melt, they don't have anywhere to live." Luke noticed, "I made a tiny hole with my finger!" Opportunity: Ask why hands melt ice. What other things melt ice? What causes ice to freeze? Where does the snow go when it melts? Where does the water go after it runs down the mountain? What do we need snow for? What do we need water for?

- As with the other classroom, the children were actively participating in dramatic play with their animals. When Gregory's bear exclaimed, "Oh, I'm sinking!" and Tilia commented, "Penguins can't get back on (when their glacier melts into the water)!" Maya quickly announced, "If yours melted, you could live on mine." As is typical with young children, they naturally want to help their friends and will share space with them.

Although it may not be feasible to build a snow globe in order to save our future snow or to wait until everything melts and then start over, it is fresh ideas like these that might spark a new train of thought with today's grown-up scientists. Our young children clearly have compassion for the earth and its inhabitants, whether they are humans, animals, or plants. Their desire and pride in helping each other and the world we share cannot be overstated. As children grow and develop, and become capable of understanding more advanced science and math concepts, it is important to remember that we can and should help them put those skills to good use. And what better ways can there be than to protect the physical environment so humans, animals, and plants can continue to coexist and hopefully thrive for many, many years to come.

I met a man with a dollar, we exchanged dollars and we still had a dollar. I met a man with an idea, we exchanged ideas and now we both have two ideas.
– Unknown

MAKING PATHWAYS IN OUR BRAINS

It was Morning Meeting in our classroom. I was telling the kids about the Learning and the Brain Conference I had attended the previous week in San Francisco. I told them that one thing I learned about was how to play games one way, then change the rules to make it trickier. I explained that this change helps teach our brains to make more pathways. We imagined that our brains were full of tall grass. As we make pathways, the grass gets squashed down. Pretty soon our path becomes a wide sidewalk, then a small road, and finally a superhighway so our ideas can ZOOM around in our brains. The children were very psyched to play!

One simple game was to have me clap my hands one time and have the children copy me. Then I'd clap two times and have the children copy me. I interchanged the claps for about a minute. The Trailblazers, regardless of age, were able to understand the rules and follow them.

Then I changed the rules so when I clapped one time, the children then had to clap two times. Conversely, when I clapped two times, the children had to clap once. This was much more difficult for all of the children, especially the three and four year olds.

- Most of the children clapped according to the rules of the original game.

- One child clapped continuously.

- Some of the older children knew the pattern had changed, but their first instinct was to copy the original pattern. But then they would alter the clap and do the clap as instructed (i.e. copied, hesitated, clapped again).

- Sara J. was concentrating very intensely and trying very hard to do the patterns. She would exclaim, "Let's do it again!" every time I would pause or stop the game. All of the children cheered when I told them we would continue to play more games like this one. Julia said, "Yeah, because fast pathways are how you get your brain full!"

Specifically, this activity is a way to help develop executive function in the brain. Executive function develops in the prefrontal cortex of the brain. It refers to the development of attention, willpower, resolution of conflicts, focused attention, working memory, and self-regulation. Executive control is also related to effortful control, or the ability to delay a reward, suppress inappropriate behavior, and do something you do not want to do. As you can see, this process is a very important aspect of learning that should not be overlooked!

EMPOWERING THE CHILDREN

- Play the above clapping game. Alter it by tapping, snapping fingers, etc.
- Walk while carrying a bell, trying not to let it ring.
- Play "Simon Says."
- Play "Head/Toes" (touch head or toes when named; then change rules so you now touch the opposite when named).
- Sort the same items by different attributes. For example, sort counting bears by color; then sort the same bears by size.
- Discuss scenarios such as:

▶ A raccoon has surgery and a sack of smelly stuff is put in its body. The raccoon is trained to squirt out when mad.... Is it a raccoon or a skunk?

▶ A puppet puts a snack in the refrigerator; then someone moves it to the cabinet. The puppet returns. Where will the puppet look for the snack?

> **If you only have a hammer, you tend to see every problem as a nail.**
> **– Abraham Maslow**

EVERY VOTE COUNTS!

Have you noticed that the rhetoric that children hear adults using as they try to solve problems and discuss issues about societal issues is often negative? This negativity is especially prevalent during election season. Political debates and commercials are on TV, and many adult discussions revolve around political issues. Unfortunately, the debates are seldom the types of discussions we want our children to hear. There is name-calling, yelling at times, and it seems everyone talks but no one listens to anyone else. What is a parent or an educator to do?

EMPOWERING THE CHILDREN

The smart thing to do is to take advantage of the situation to talk about what the adults are doing wrong and what they are doing right. For instance:

• What words could they have used instead?

• How would you feel if someone talked to you like that?

- How would you feel if someone talked about you like that?

- Discuss tone of voice, volume of voice, and body language. Practice it with each other to see how it feels. Talk about the effects on your body when you are attacked verbally (stomach hurts, heart races, scared feeling inside, etc.). Even little guys can get the gist of it, even if they don't have the terms down (mad voice, for example).

- Don't forget to practice and discuss better ways to do it. Remind them that adults sometimes make poor choices, too, and people can learn better ways of doing things even if they are 100 years old!

Another important lesson in a democratic society is to teach children the history and importance of voting, but in a concrete way so they can understand. I think one of the sad tragedies in the U.S. is the lack of voting by eligible adults and the way we complain about our own personal situations without doing something to change them. These two things are connected, and it is imperative to teach children that they have the power to make their voices heard as a community and in their individual lives.

Different from the decision not to vote is the current political climate that makes it difficult or impossible for eligible voters to cast their votes due to voter suppression laws. These citizens can't utilize their right and privilege to shape policies for themselves and others. We need to remember, even if we do not "win," we need to utilize our privilege of voting to express what we believe in, to express what we think is important, and to ensure all U.S. citizens can as well.

VOTING FOR "TODAY'S FAVORITE COLOR"

Here is just one of several techniques that worked for me when I talked about voting with groups of preschoolers as young as three years old:

1. Cut out a variety of squares of colored paper, making sure you have included enough squares so each child can have his or her favorite color. Have a box or container into which the colored squares can be placed. (This is your voting booth!)

- Have each child pick his or her favorite color from the variety of colored paper squares.

- Explain how we are going to vote for "Today's Favorite Color" by having each child put his or her square in the box.

- Vote.

- Count or tally the results. The color with the most votes is declared the winner.

- Write down the winning color using the corresponding colored marker so everyone can clearly see/understand which color won the election. Explain again that this is the voting process.

- Return the colored papers to the children, telling them they will get to vote in a few different elections, and we will record the results every time.

2. Next, tell the children a long time ago, the only people in the U.S. who could vote were men with white skin who owned property (houses). This information brings up the issue of classifying kids by skin color. Research shows that children are already aware of these differences at age two, the same age they notice who is a boy and who is a girl.

The first thing worth mentioning when talking to kids about skin color is that no color of skin is better or worse than any other color of skin. We just happen to get our color from our mom and our dad, and they got it from their moms and dads. (As a separate activity, you could do some color mixing with paints or watercolors. To keep it close to skin tones, use white paint and add drips of pink, brown, yellow, and black, and see what happens!)

When comparing hands/skin color, comment on the lovely shades of peach, bread, cinnamon, etc. Ask the kids what color they would give their own skin color. Discuss whether or not anyone is really white. Since no one is truly white like a piece of paper, explain that the term "white" person is just a description someone came up with a long time ago because it was easier for that person to say "white" skin or "black" skin like we have a simple name for "boys" or "girls."

Then, go on to ask whether it makes sense to say someone can't do something because of the color of his or her skin (run, jump, color, read books, play with you, etc.). Use the people the children know as examples.

Next, you can ask whether the kids think it made sense that a long time ago some people were told they couldn't vote because of their skin color. They will gladly tell you how ludicrous this notion is to them.

Finally, tell them it is okay to tell other people to "Stop and be fair" if they notice someone discriminating against someone because of who he is (boy, girl, white, black, big, small, slow, fast, etc.).

- Tell the girls they don't get to vote this time. Ask whether they think this is fair or not. Why or why not? Discuss.

- Compare the skin color of the boys' skin to determine who is white and tell the others they can't vote this time. Ask if they think this is fair or not. Why or why not? Discuss.

- Tell half of the white boys they do not own a house (for pretend) so they can't vote. Ask whether they think this is fair or not. Why or why not? Discuss.

- Finally, vote and tally the results. Declare a winner and write down the winning color using the corresponding colored marker so everyone can clearly see/understand which color won the election.

3. Then, tell the children that people decided this situation was not fair. They changed the laws so all men, no matter what color they were, could vote. But women could still not vote.

- Tell them all the boys can vote, but still no girls. Ask whether or not they think this is fair. Why or why not? Discuss.

- Finally, vote and tally the results. Declare a winner and write down the winning color using the corresponding colored marker so everyone can clearly see/understand which color won the election.

4. At last, everyone can vote.

- Ask whether or not they think this is fair. Why or why not? Discuss.

- Review the results from the first election.

5. Compare and contrast the winners each time. (In my experience, in a random group of eighteen children, a different color won each time! We saw, by illustration of the differences in colors voted for and the different results each time, how voting outcomes could be affected strictly based on who could vote.)

6. Tell the kids there is one last thing to know. Just because people can vote, doesn't mean they *do* vote. Tell them how sometimes an adult might think that since a lot of other people will be voting for the same people they would vote for, they might actually think it doesn't matter whether they vote. Or maybe they are too tired that day. Or they might think it is too hard to decide. So they don't vote.

- Ask whether or not they think this is fair. Why or why not? Discuss.

- Most groups are able to come up with a version of "If you don't vote, you get what you get, and you don't throw a fit!" You can't complain about the results because you chose not to vote.

- Practice another election in which some kids choose not to vote for some reason. Record the results using the corresponding colored marker so everyone can clearly see/understand which color won the election.

- Compare and contrast these results to those when everyone could vote. Are they different?

When it is election time, please use your voice. It does count. Remember, less than 1 percent of the U.S. population was able to force political changes such as giving us civil rights and providing women with the right to vote. The whole country was changed for the better because those people became involved. Today, many states make it even easier, like the state of Washington where I reside, by allowing citizens to vote by mail from the convenience of their homes. Get involved. Care. Vote! Your children are watching how you solve problems.

Note: Although adults vote for political candidates, children don't always get an equal vote at home or at school. Parents and teachers should listen to children's viewpoints and arguments in many situations, but then the adults should make the final decision. Telling children how you made your decision helps them cope with results they may not like.

SUMMARY

Problem-solving is a crucial skill that will empower children throughout their lives. Remember to:

- State or define the problem.
- Supply the facts as needed.

- Ask the kids for their thoughts, suggestions, and ideas. There are no right or wrong answers, only possibilities.

- Experiment with your kids. Help them to try out their hypotheses about the world.

- Evaluate their hypotheses. Did their experiments work? Why or why not?

- Chapter 3 has a section specifically about bullying behaviors. Please refer to it for information on how to handle these situations.

CELEBRATING PROBLEM-SOLVING
THROUGHOUT THE YEAR

★

January: Get Organized Month

                Self-Help Group Awareness Month

                Hunt for Happiness Week
                (Last full week)

February: Great Backyard Bird Count
                (Third weekend)

                Single-Tasking Day (19)

                Secondhand Wardrobe Week
                (Last week)

March: International Ideas Month

                Telecommuter Appreciation Week
                (First week)

                What If Cats and Dogs Had Opposable
                Thumbs Day (3)

                Dream 2013 Day (11)

                Sherlock Holmes Weekend (Third
                weekend, also first weekend
                of November)

                National Day of Unplugging
                (Last weekend)

                What You Think Upon Grows Day (31)

April:	Screen Free Week (Last few days in April through early May)
May:	Love a Tree Day (16)
June:	Let It Go Day (23)
July:	National Make a Difference to Children Month
	World Population Day (11)
August:	Sneak Some Zucchini Onto Your Neighbor's Porch Day (8)
September:	Hunger Action Month
	International Strategic Thinking Month
	Swap Ideas Day (10)
	National Indoor Plant Week (Third week)
	International Day for the Preservation of the Ozone Layer (16)
	International Coastal Cleanup (21)
	International Day of Peace (21)
	National Keep Kids Creative Week (Last week)
October:	Gandhi's Birthday (2)
	International Day of Nonviolence (2)
	Kids' Goal-Setting Week (First full week)

World Habitat Day (7)

World Rainforest Week (First full week)

Evaluate Your Life Day (19)

November: Sherlock Holmes Weekend (First, also third weekend of March)

Use Your Common Sense Day (4)

Election Day (6)

America Recycles Day (15)

Family Volunteer Day (23)

December: Make Up Your Mind Day (31)

No Interruptions Day (31)

Chapter Five

Community Building

★

Never doubt that a small group of thoughtful, committed citizens can change the world; indeed, it's the only thing that ever has.
– Margaret Mead

HOMELESS IN SEATTLE: PART 1

The following events occurred September 22, 2011 in my Trailblazer Classroom.

My friend and colleague, Patty Hatfield, would occasionally surprise me with different materials she'd come across that she thought my classroom kids would enjoy—wiggly eyes for art projects, plastic bottle caps for the sensory table, and books that were beyond the scope of the toddlers and twos she was currently teaching. On this day, she brought in a book she was sure my group of preschoolers would really connect with. The kids were captivated by *The Teddy Bear*, a story about a boy who loses his favorite teddy bear, which is then found in a garbage can and loved by a homeless man. In the story, the boy finds the teddy bear a year later on a park bench. When the boy hears the man crying and searching for his missing teddy bear as the boy is walking away, he returns the bear to the crying man. David McPhail's book is a beautiful story that talks about a homeless person without even using the word homeless. My preschoolers saw homeless people all the time in their daily lives since they attended day care in the city and many of them were city dwellers, just like many other children in our country. This book was a great way to begin to discuss this issue in a humane way and to get children thinking about others less fortunate than themselves.

As I mentioned, the children were completely transfixed by this story. You could have heard a pin drop as I read this lovely book to them for the first of many times. When the story ended, we had a very heartwarming discussion about it. Some of the details of that discussion revolved around cause and effect ("The boy lost his bear because it fell on the floor so his parents couldn't see it." While eating at a diner, the boy falls asleep, knocking his bear under the table accidentally.), defining new vocabulary ("What is a dumpster?"), and thinking about what types of things the man might look for in the garbage cans while he was "working" ("Food, a cozy scarf"; "Maybe a plastic bag to keep his treasures dry and clean, or cardboard to shelter him from the wind or rain.").

What made such a huge impression on me, however, was the ease with which the children demonstrated compassion for others and recognized what is fair or the right thing to do. When we were exploring why we thought the homeless man cried when he thought his teddy bear was gone, my insightful four-year-old friend Julia exclaimed, "Maybe even adults get lonely too! The teddy bear was his friend and he missed his friend." Wow!

These young people also noticed and asked why the parents in the story walked away quickly when they saw the homeless man walking toward them, even though the book did not state this specifically (the parents suggested they hurry up as the man was walking toward them). We decided that sometimes people don't know what to say or do when someone else needs help, looks dirty, or needs a bath. Or maybe the parents felt nervous because parents are always wanting to keep their kids safe and they didn't know the man.

A bit of a debate began when I asked the children why they thought the boy decided to give the bear back to the man. Chen began with "To make the man happy." His friends agreed that this was correct, until Julia interjected, "But it really was the boy's bear first." Issues about ownership and fairness were added to the discussion. After some debate, I refocused the group by asking whether they thought the boy had other toys to play with at his house. Elizabeth exclaimed, "Yes! So he shared it with the man. He didn't need so many toys!" Bingo!

We wrapped up our conversation after Elizabeth and Maya commented that the boy was smiling as he walked away because he felt happy after helping someone.

Finally, we made a list of ideas, including what each of us might do if we saw someone who was lonely, cold, hungry, or tired like the man in the book. Noah suggested giving him apples and water since those are healthy foods, while Tommy proposed bringing him to his house for pizza and apple juice. While that is a generous idea, I wanted the kids to know that they could help people without bringing them to their homes. I relayed the story about a former student of mine named Quinn who would keep boxes of granola bars in his car. When Quinn and his parents would see someone who looked hungry, they would stop the car and offer the person a granola bar.

This also seemed like the perfect time to reiterate that sometimes just saying "Hello" to people or giving them a smile can also make them feel happy. Lots of people look away from others who look dirty or maybe smell bad because they can't take a bath very often. A little kindness can really brighten their day.

At that point, Cameron declared that he was not sure what he would do if he saw a real homeless person. I reassured him that it was okay not to know; it's good just to think about it in case it ever happens to him.

Jessica and I have had the Trailblazers put on a play for the past four years as a way to combine social awareness and civic responsibility with the creativity, language skills, and confidence required to perform in front of a group. Because of the response of the children to *The Teddy Bear,* we performed a play with the same name in the Fall of 2011 as a way to raise money and awareness for homeless individuals and families in our city of Seattle.

"The process of really being with other people in a safe, supportive situation can actually change who we think we are.... And as we grow closer to the essence of who we are, we tend to take more responsibility for our neighbors and our planet.
– Bill Kauth

HOMELESS IN SEATTLE: PART 2

The following events occurred on December 13, 2011 in my Trailblazer Classroom.

This morning was an important and special morning for the Trailblazers. We were having Isaiah John, a homeless newspaper vendor, come to visit our classroom before our first performance of *The Teddy Bear*. We wanted to raise money for the homeless people in Seattle and learn more about what it meant to be homeless after reading this great storybook a number of weeks ago. We raised approximately $325 in donations from the performance. Adults were not the only ones who generously shared their money for our cause; we had children, as young as three years old, from other classrooms bring baggies of coins to our class after watching the play and having "Question and Answer" time. Many piggy banks were opened by child-request!

As a teacher, I have learned the importance of making experiences as concrete as possible for young children. If you are learning about building bridges, it is best to have blocks and other building materials to experiment with as you invent your own structures for vehicles to cross over and under. So it follows that when learning about homeless individuals, it is best to have a person who is currently living on the streets talk to you directly. I began my search for a representative of the community who would be willing and able to talk to a group of children, but who would also be a person who would be a good match for us to have in our classroom. After all, we screen volunteers and clear other visitors who approach us to spend time with our kids and in our schools. So how could I find the right person?

In a moment of serendipity, I purchased an issue of *Real Change*, a local newspaper that reports on community issues and is sold by vendors who happen to be homeless. As I was reading it, I came across the "Vendor of the Week." Isaiah John was the featured vendor, and his unique personality came to life in that article in the newspaper he himself sells to make a living. Isaiah recognized that he needed a novel approach to get people interested in his papers, and since he had always loved singing, he decided that music was his ticket to interacting with passersby. He inserted the name of the paper into his catalogue of over 100 well-loved songs, creating fun tunes such as "Rudolph the Real Change Reindeer," to get people to buy a newspaper from him. Isaiah clearly worked hard, and he sold more than 600 papers a month. I knew Isaiah was the type of person who might be a good fit for my Trailblazers.

After work one day, I went to Isaiah's street corner with a copy of *The Teddy Bear*, along with a copy of his article from *Real Change* and a copy of an invitation to be our special guest at the premiere performance of our play. Isaiah was very interested in our project, although he was a little surprised at learning the ages of my friends. But he quickly discovered that body size has no correlation to the size of one's heart.

The night before the big day, Isaiah surprised me by calling to confirm the date, time, and location of the event, and to express his excitement about meeting the children. He also wanted to make sure it was okay if he brought the children candy canes as a little treat. Isaiah was already breaking down my own preconceived ideas about homeless people by finding a phone to confirm his commitment to us. Instead of focusing on his own plight, he was thinking about other people and spending his money on them. I had a great feeling about the next day.

Isaiah was due to arrive at 9:30 in the morning, but he was very late. This situation helped us to understand an issue that relates to many homeless people—the lack of reliable transportation. We talked about how it was likely that Isaiah did not have a car, so he was probably trying to find a bus or was walking a long way to get to our school. Isaiah eventually was able to call to say he was lost and in a taxicab trying to find his way to our school.

Isaiah arrived around 10:30 while we were outside, running off a little steam before our show started. To the delight and surprise of the children, he was decked out in a fantastic elf costume! After greeting the children warmly, he asked me whether I could show him where to put his belongings, which consisted of a backpack and a plastic garbage bag of other possessions. While I took him to the classroom, Jessica answered the numerous questions from the children about why he brought all of his things with him and why he wanted a safe place for them.

I was humbled and in awe of the lengths Isaiah went to in order to get to our school. I was also shocked that he would spend money on taxi fare, candy canes, and a holiday costume to attend our event. We wanted to share with him because he was homeless, and he kept sharing to be with us! Fortunately, he allowed Jessica and I to reimburse him for his taxi and provide him with a "Speaker's Fee" since he took time off from selling his papers to be an important part of our morning.

When Isaiah returned outside, he sang "Jingle Bells" to the children. Three-year-old Julien stood close by, and when Isaiah finished singing, Julien said, "You know, I know 'Jingle Bells,' too!" When Isaiah asked Julien whether he wanted to sing it with him, Julien replied "YES!" They sang together and other children and teachers joined in as well. Isaiah then passed out candy canes to the children as they thanked him.

Time was flying so we quickly returned to the classroom for a quick meeting with Isaiah in the role of the teacher. He told the kids a funny story about how he used to be an elf at the North Pole, but he really wanted to be a singer so he came to Seattle. Now he sings and sells his newspapers.

We had time for a quick dose of reality as Isaiah told us he was very fortunate because he had a sleeping bag and a blanket to keep him warm. He told us that many people are not that lucky. He also told us he ate at the soup kitchens many times a week but not every day. He helped us expand upon our current knowledge about soup kitchens by telling us that everyone stood in line and waited patiently to get their warm food.

Isaiah also told the Trailblazers that one of the best things they could do to help people who are homeless is to smile and say, "Hi." He said lots of people are afraid of the homeless, but homeless people like to be friendly too. The Trailblazers told him how Julia helped us realize that "Adults can be lonely too." He definitely agreed.

I think Isaiah's positive self-esteem was good for the children to see. He told them, "Sometimes life is hard, but you try hard and follow your dreams." He didn't feel sorry for himself or make himself seem incapable of having a positive, happy life. In fact, he seemed to expect it and radiated joy. I also liked that he was personable and fun with the children; they loved him and thought he was very funny. I hope they will remember their friend who sleeps outside in a sleeping bag and eats at soup kitchens as they get older.

Finally it was time for the play to begin! Many parents and family members had arrived as well as children from other classrooms. We introduced our special guest and then the show started. Each child had more than one important part to play during the two times we acted out the story. These young actors enjoyed playing multiple parts and working behind the scenes. I was once again impressed by the Trailblazers' openness to new experiences, their hard work, and their ability to step into the spotlight and be gracious hosts. I was so proud of each of them as individuals and as a team of friends.

After the play was over, many of the parents stayed to talk with Isaiah. Handshakes and hugs were plentiful. Julien's family gave Isaiah a ride to the *Real Change* newspaper office so he could pick up his newspapers, beginning his day's work.

Although I wasn't surprised, it was wonderful to see all of the parents and family members reaching out to Isaiah and treating him so respectfully. I am confident these children will turn out just like their parents, and our world will be better for it!

As Isaiah left he said, "This is just the beginning, Karen. I can feel it! Can I use you and Jessica as references someday? I'd also be happy to come back any time you'd like."

Update:

- Isaiah had a few more visits to our classroom during this past school year. One time, he brought two little candy canes for each child, one for the child and one for the child to give to another person who was not in our classroom. He wanted the children to know, "The best thing about presents is giving them."

- Isaiah spent Christmas with Jessica and her family. They provided him with a shower, clean clothes, a sofa to sleep on, and some treats from our classroom friends. Isaiah, of course, snuck out early in the morning to purchase goodies for breakfast, which he helped to prepare for the family.

- Isaiah came to the classroom without his elf makeup and costume on, giving us step-by-step instructions in "How to Become an Elf." This experience was especially exciting and funny because a few of the kids did not realize that Isaiah was wearing fake ears and a fake nose on his first visit to see us. They just thought he had big ears and a big nose!

- The Trailblazers talked about Isaiah often, included him in their artwork, and remembered him on their birthdays. He has had more than a few families search him out on the street so their child could give him a cupcake on the child's birthday. Because the best thing about presents is giving them.

Equality comes in realizing that we are all doing different jobs for a common purpose. That is the aim behind any community. The very name community means let's come together to recognize the unity. Come...unity.
– Swami Satchidananda

ACTIVITY: BREAKING OUT OF YOUR COMFORT ZONE

- What are your feelings toward those who are different from yourself?

- Do you find yourself acting or speaking differently depending on whom it is? (avoiding, more or less helpful, anxious, etc?)

- Challenge yourself next time by stepping out of your comfort zone. Say hello to someone you would normally ignore; stop to help someone in need.

- How do you feel after this new experience?

EMPOWERING THE CHILDREN:

What types of people are your children interested in? Whom do they have questions or concerns about?

- Answer their questions, finding and providing accurate facts for them.

- Focus on similarities between objects and people instead of the differences.

  ▸ Read *Shades of People* by Shelly Rotner and Sheila M. Kelly to appreciate our different skin colors. Compare the skin color of your family and friends, giving them beautiful names like peach, honey, cinnamon, and cocoa.

  ▸ Read *The Crayon Box That Talked* by Shane Derolf and Michael Letzig to reinforce the message "We are a box of crayons, each one of us unique. But when we get together...The picture is complete." Each person is necessary to make our community whole.

- Have a project that you do with your children.

  ▸ Collect food, make decorations, clean a room, bake the food. Invite guests over for a visit. Make gifts for others.

> ### Planning for the International Day of Peace
>
> The International Day of Peace is September 21. It is a day celebrated around the world to observe peace within and among nations. Ideally, it would also be a day without violence around the world. This includes acts of war and terrorism.
>
> As you know, peace starts with one person. One act of kindness. Will you raise awareness this year? Make one person's life less lonely? Raise money for a worthy cause? What will you do to take a stand on September 21st to make the world a better place? Let's use this special event as a reason to begin an on-going campaign for peace!

KIDS MAKING A MORE PEACEFUL WORLD

In Seattle's neighborhood of South Lake Union, a group of three and four year olds talked with their classroom teachers about what peace means to them and how to build community, locally and around the world in honor of the International Day of Peace. When one of the parents heard about the activity, she wondered whether children of this age could even understand the concept of peace. The teacher responded, "Absolutely. Just look at their answers! You just relate the concept to the world that your child lives in, which for the most part is school and home."

These are the children's ideas for making a more peaceful world:

- Alex: They (people who need a place to live) could go to my home to sleep.

- Anvi: If nobody hits, pushes, or bites people, then that's peaceful.

- Beck: I left the caterpillar alone and then it became a butterfly.

- Cora: Getting a Band-Aid for someone's ouchie.

- Chiyo: We could share pianos.

- Dash: When mommies or little girls are sad, you can put a Band-Aid on them and hug them.

- Jack: Be nice to animals. (Jack also explained that his family once saw a baby squirrel and they knew it was NOT good to touch it because its mommy might not feed it anymore.)

- Sabine: You can share your house with someone.

- Louis: You can share with a friend and they will share with you.

- Ella: When people fight I would tell them to share.

- Ellen: When something is wrong, there are people that can help you.

- Sahana: You can paint a picture for someone.

- Madeline: My mommy has an ouchie and I share my Baa-baa sheep.

Like their teachers, I also believe these children understand the concept of peace. To them, it means sharing space and belongings, treating each other's bodies with respect, and allowing nature's animals and plants to grow and live in natural settings without humans encroaching on their environment. It means giving aid and comfort to the injured, reminding those who are fighting to stop, and asking for help when you need it (and expecting to be helped in return!). And let's not forget the power of beauty to warm and calm the heart, whether it is music or art.

So let's all share pianos, make a picture for someone, and give comfort to the next person we see who needs it, whomever he or she may be! And when we see our next butterfly fluttering around us, let's give thanks to all the people who allowed that caterpillar to reach its potential and become that butterfly! And, hopefully, that butterfly will remind us of the gift that each individual person is, and with proper care and feeding, will become a peaceful, happy, and beautiful member of our society.

Thank you for participating today and every day, my young friends. Your kind hearts are the building blocks that will help us construct a better tomorrow!

A candle loses nothing by lighting another candle.
– Proverb

EMPOWERING THE CHILDREN

One of the biggest parts of community building is making sure there is respect for the people, belongings, and space the group shares. So it is paramount to make sure interactions are socially acceptable.

- Take advantage of the situation to talk about what is happening that needs to be changed. For instance:
  - ▸ What words could they have used instead?
  - ▸ How would you feel if someone talked to you like that?

▸ Discuss tone of voice, volume of voice, and body language.

▸ Practice it with each other to see how it feels.

⯈ Talk about the effects on your body when you are attacked verbally (stomach hurts, heart races, scared feeling inside, etc.) or physically. Even little guys can get the gist of it, even if they don't have the terms down (mad voice, for example).

▸ Discuss better ways to do it. Remind them that adults sometimes make poor choices, too, and people can learn better ways of doing things even if they are 100 years old!

- Provide a name for your group and talk about it proudly, not as a means of exclusion but inclusion. For example, your surname, classroom name, city, or a descriptive name such as "Nature Lovers" or "Garden Tenders."

- Have a "Wall of Kindness." Hang notes or drawings of appreciation in a designated area for all in the group to see. If your children cannot write, write their messages of gratitude for them.

- Hang a sign on the door to remind others they are entering "The Kindness Zone." It could say "Welcome to the Kindness Zone. Enter with a smile."

ADULTS AS LEADERS

Parents and teachers can fall into the trap of trying to be equally fair to everyone, leading to indecisiveness and inaction. Please notice the difference between being neutral and being an engaged leader. Listen in an unbiased manner to draw your children out, but do not forget to lead them down the path. Demonstrate how individuals in a group can disagree and work through problems. Unite all parties in your community by allowing them to bring their unique strengths to the table and contribute in their own way. Allow them to feel both responsibility for and success achieved in the family, classroom, or other community group.

Be kind to unkind people. They need it the most.
– Ashleigh Brilliant

SUMMARY

Feeling that you are part of a community is an important part of being a happy and successful person. Loneliness can lead to depression, physical illness, bullying behaviors, and a host of other social ills. People on the fringes of society are more likely to be homeless or in prison. You can set your children up to have a strong foundation for success by focusing on their ability to be a part of and build our community locally and around the world. You can begin with your home community and classroom community and expand outwards.

CELEBRATING COMMUNITY BUILDING
THROUGHOUT THE YEAR

★

January: International Year of Water Cooperation

                  Celebration of Life Month
                  (new beginnings)

                  40th Anniversary of National
                  Nothing Day (16)

February: Plant the Seeds of Greatness Month

                  National Pancake Week (Week of
                  Ash Wednesday)

                  National Have-a-Heart Day (14)

March: Dr. Seuss' (Theodor Geisel) Birthday (2)

                  Peace Corps Day (5)

                  Won't You Be My Neighbor Day (20)

                  Week of Solidarity with Peoples
                  Struggling Against Racism and Racial
                  Discrimination (21-27)

                  International Goof-Off Day (22)

                  Earth Hour (30): @ 8:30 p.m. local;
                  1 hour lights off

April: Community Service Month

                  National Rebuilding Month

                  Community Spirit Days (1-30)

National Fun Day (1)

National Love Your Produce Manager Day (2)

Weed Out Hate: Sow the Seeds of Peace Day (3)

National Love Our Children Day (6)

National Siblings Day (10)

Week of the Young Child (varies)

National High Five Day (18)

National Volunteer Week (varies)

Screen-Free Week starts (End of April through early May)

May: Older Americans Month

Join Hands Day (4)

National Dance Day (4)

World Give Day (4)

No Socks Day (8)

National Family Month (May 12-June 16)

National Police Week (Week of the 15th)

Transportation Week (Mid-month)

International Day of Families (15)

International New Friends, Old Friends
Week (18-25)

Visit Your Relatives Day (18)

National Backyard Games Week
(Week before Memorial Day)

Brother's Day (24)

June: National Hunger Awareness Month

International Children's Day (1)

Hunger Day (6)

Family History Day (14)

Great American Backyard Campout (22)

National Handshake Day (27)

July: National Ice Cream Month

National Make a Difference to
Children Month

Father-Daughter Take a Walk
Together Day (7)

National Ice Cream Day (21)

Cousins Day (24)

One Voice (26): synchronized reading;
www.peacedome.org

August: Sister's Day (4)

Weird Contest Week (Mid-month)

Best Friend's Day (15)

World Humanitarian Day (19)

Be an Angel Day (22)

Be Kind to Humankind Week
(Last week)

Kiss-and-Make-Up Day (25)

September: Million Minute Family Challenge
(September 1-December 31)

National Grandparents' Day (8)

National Hug Your Hound Day (8)

International Talk Like a Pirate Day (19)

Family Day—A Day to Eat Dinner
with Your Children (23)

International Day of Peace (21)

October: Million Minute Family Challenge
(September 1-December 31)

International Day of Non-Violence/
Gandhi's Birthday (2)

Intergeneration Month

National Bake and Decorate Month

National Popcorn Poppin' Month

World Humanitarian Action Day (8)

National Character Counts Week
(Third week)

Universal Music Day (12)

National Take Your Parents to Lunch
Day (16)

World Food Day (16)

November: Million Minute Family Challenge
(September 1-December 31)

Homemade Bread Day (17)

World Hello Day (21)

National Family Week (Last week)

National Game and Puzzle Week
(Last week)

December: Million Minute Family challenge
(September1-December 31)

Universal Hour of Peace (31): @
11:30 p.m. local for 1 hour

Chapter Six

Learning About the World

★

Knowledge is like a garden: if it is not cultivated, it cannot be harvested.
– African Proverb

When we consider all of the things children need to learn about the world they live in, our brains usually jump to the endless facts, figures, and examples that have to do with traditional school education—math, science, reading, writing, and social studies. While these are undoubtedly important, what I'd like to focus on are those more subtle lessons, those lessons that are genuinely powerful in giving our children the successful lives they desire now and as adults.

I am a very strong advocate of education, and I do not want to be misunderstood on this point. But I strongly believe that we can set the stage for how our children are able to learn in their world, allowing them more success. For example, let's imagine Anne is five years old and loves penguins. A parent could purchase penguin stuffed animals for birthday gifts or maybe give Anne a storybook with a penguin as a character, all of which she would love. Maybe Anne would learn about penguins at school sometime.

Another option would be to ask Anne what she knows about penguins and what she wants to know about penguins. Then start learning!

- Have a penguin week:
  - ▸ Eat fish for dinner.
  - ▸ Balance a ball on your feet just like a penguin parent balances its baby penguin egg and little baby.
  - ▸ Just like the mother and father penguins take turns caring for the penguin egg and babies, perhaps you could have a mom date and a dad date with each of your children.
  - ▸ How do penguin parents know which baby is theirs? By the sound of their voices! Record your family members' voices and see whether your children can figure out who is who.
  - ▸ Learn about penguin environments. Can you help the polar ice caps in some way?
  - ▸ Draw pictures in black and white.
  - ▸ Slide on your stomachs to the bedroom at night.

The gist is to apply learning to everyday life by making it real and relatable to your unique children. You can also send the message that your children can make a difference in the world and today. If they are passionate about monkeys, help them get involved in saving the rainforest, for example.

I'm also a huge advocate for play, especially open-ended, no-right-way, make-it-up-as-you-go play. When children have unstructured time to explore materials (blocks, people figures, animals, etc.), they make up their own stories and are able to come up with their own problems and solutions to them. With a Batman doll, the role is always the same, the kids say the words they know Batman says, and they don't vary their play from the script. (In Chapter 8 we will discuss superhero play in more depth.)

We need to find out what our children are interested in so we can take their learning further. Using real items in addition to toys is helpful. Remember, children's activities are real to them. Play and learning define their lives. Let's help them make an impact.

REDESIGNING THE PLAYGROUND

A few years ago, four-year-old Cady, who was in my preschool classroom, was sitting rather glumly in the art area. I asked her what was bothering her. She said, "I wish our playground was more funner." I asked her to tell me what she meant by "funner," and she proceeded to tell me things like: absolutely NO wood chips, a place to grow and pick flowers, maybe an apple tree that chipmunks could live in, and a butterfly garden. Cady was very interested in nature—grass, animals, hills, natural landscaping, and opportunities to dig in the dirt. This response did not surprise me too much since Cady was often pretending to be a "furry white cat-squirrel with a bushy tail and wet nose" or some other interesting animal hybrid.

Her classmate James, also age four, overheard our conversation and said he thought there should also be poles to which they could attach different flags to suit their moods (pirate, space, etc.), ladders to climb, tunnels to go through, and structures of multiple levels to hide in and to get privacy for important meetings. I knew that preschoolers needed their own hideouts, but I didn't realize they also wanted their own meeting rooms! Further proof that they want to do the same things their parents do!

I happened to know that our playground was going to be redone in the following year, so I thought this would be a fantastic opportunity to find out directly from the beneficiaries of the playground what they would enjoy and what they felt they needed. So I asked Cady and James to draw or paint their "Best Playground Ever" for me. We would use their thoughts to begin a brainstorming session with the rest of the class a bit later.

After Jessica and I gathered the kids for morning meeting/circle time, James and Cady showed them their pictures and asked for their ideas as well. The kids quickly volunteered their ideas: fire poles, forts, monkey bars, slides, gardens, and trees in addition to the ideas Cady and James mentioned. In fact, they were so excited about a "Best Playground Ever" that they wanted to go immediately to the art area to begin designing! So we took advantage of their enthusiasm, ironically canceling outside time, and put them to work.

Over the next week, these fired-up three to five year olds made 3-D models of their ideas. Here are a few of them:

- A two-story fort complete with ladder.

- A flag pole with a "car" flag that waves in the wind.

- A garden trellis for plants to grow on.

- A covered slide that doubles as a hideout.

- An apple tree with a hole for chipmunks to live in.

Next on the agenda? We set a date to have three of the children meet with the six board members and parents who made up the Playground Committee. Cady, James, and Harry met in a conference room, describing what they liked and did not like about the current playground. Then they shared the models and their vision for the "Best Playground Ever."

I was so impressed with these young children's poise and confidence as they rose to the occasion to make their views known! They were calm, cool, and collected in a way that would be the envy of many adults. The committee members said they would take the children's suggestions into consideration.

Unfortunately for my playground designers, they would be in kindergarten before our playground renovation would be finished. As a classroom, we decided to do what we could to bring their ideas and concepts to our old playground now. They worked so hard; it was important to Jessica and me for the children to experience the feeling of follow-through and results!

We made "flags" out of cardboard and plastic (science experiment!) and attached them to the playground fence and to old Christmas tree trunks that our assistant director brought to school for us.

We took sheets, tarps, and blocks outside to try to build various shelters. We took stuffed animals outside for "wildlife." We took big cardboard boxes outside to use as tunnels until the rain required us to recycle them.

In the end, even though this group of children did not get to have a brand new playground of their own, I think we did end up with the "Best Playground Ever." Why? Because the children learned that they didn't have to wait to be adults to make a difference. They could visualize their ideas and make them concrete. They could share their ideas with adults so the adults could understand what was important to them. They were empowered to make changes to their environment so it would better meet their needs. They didn't feel sad that the new playground was for someone else. They made their very own "Best Playground Ever."

EMPOWERING THE CHILDREN

Numerous activities can occur during a project such as this, thus the possibilities for learning are endless! A few things we discovered as we designed our dream playground included how to:

- Challenge our fine motor skills. Cutting, drawing, gluing, connecting, and painting opportunities were abundant.

- Carry out long-term project planning, including following directions and breaking larger tasks into smaller steps.

- Measure with rulers, shoes, blocks, animals. (Anything that can be lined up can be used to measure something. For example, one table length = 6 rulers = 24 blocks = 48 cars.) Compare and contrast measurements.

- Count or sort money for purchasing the plastic required for flag making.

- Explore the idea of gravity as we tried to figure out how to connect tree trunks to the fence without them falling down.

- Compare and contrast the effects of water on cardboard vs. plastic flags.

- Speak in front of a group.

- Carry heavy tree trunks. Teamwork is a necessity!

- Encourage grown-ups to respond to kids making plans to make a difference. Their encouragement, time spent listening to the children, and time spent taking them seriously helped to reinforce and reaffirm the children's efforts and value to their larger community.

**There can be no knowledge without emotion.
We may be aware of a truth, yet until we have
felt its force, it is not ours.
– Anonymous**

SOFIA'S PEACE CORPS

Sofia, a petite, curly-topped three year old, had an enormous impact on our classroom when she told us she was going on vacation to the place her mother, Carolyn, lived while in the Peace Corps. Carolyn had spent seven years in a village in the Dominican Republic, living in a small hut without running water and electricity. Sofia, her parents, and her older brother were going to visit Carolyn's former village over the month of December for a real adventure.

Because the children in the classroom were very interested in this trip, we set up a time for Carolyn to come to our room and share with us her photos from her life in the Dominican Republic. We found the island (shared with Haiti) on the globe and proceeded to see many amazing things:

- Children were very dusty and dirty, with little clothing.
- The school was an open shack with dirt floors and wooden benches. No supplies were apparent.
- A few children were playing with the inner tube from a bicycle. We saw no other toys.
- Children had to help carry water every day, balancing water jugs on their heads. The water source was a fifteen-minute walk.

The children, Jessica, and I were stunned. The children wanted to do *something* to help. Carolyn said she would take two extra suitcases on the trip if we wanted to send things along. Sofia would help deliver their gifts.

The children were extremely excited about this project. They wanted to "make it right" somehow. So they brought in toys, books, clothes, and coats for the friends they hadn't met. Sofia's family delivered the gifts, and they returned with photos of the children wearing the clothes and playing with the toys. This made a huge impact on the kids!

EMPOWERING THE CHILDREN

Activities to extend a project such as this one include:

- Set up a dramatic play/pretend play area with props similar to those you see in the culture you are learning about. For example, we made a "lean-to" house out of cardboard, added fabric for making clothing (to tie around waists, heads), a couple of simple plates, and containers for collecting and carrying water on our heads; artificial leaves and vines for the jungle; a blue sheet to use for a stream; sand in bins for drawing with fingers.

- Do not focus on negatives or make it seem like poor people have horrible, worthless lives! Try not to focus on how others are different, but rather focus on how people are the same, have families who love each other, and need the same things: shelter, food, clothing, and water.

- Ask "What can we do to help families get supplies that they need?"

  ▸ Brainstorm ideas!

  ▸ Try some of the ideas in real life or pretend play to see how they work.

  ▸ Go back to the drawing board if needed.

- Introduce reduce, reuse, recycle to your home or classrooms. Instead of throwing something away, recycle it (soup can). Better yet, reuse it in a new way (soup can be decorated for a pencil holder) or avoid the waste in the first place (make homemade soup; no can!).

- Have a book exchange with your kids' friends, in the neighborhood, or classroom.
  - ▶ Everyone brings a book from home that he or she no longer reads.
  - ▶ Put all of the books on display.
  - ▶ Have the children pick a new book to take home.
- Donate toys, clothes, and food to homeless shelters and other charities.

The ability to perceive or think differently is more important than the knowledge gained.
– David Bohm

A RENAISSANCE MAN

Children are by nature curious. They want to know why the sky is blue, how to climb *up* the fire pole, and how deep the puddles are. They are also curious about other people, including their teachers. Once they realize that we really don't live at school, they want to know whether we sleep in beds (Yes!), have a car (Sometimes), and whom we live with (In my case, whether that man who sometimes picks me up from school is my daddy. Sorry, John!).

One day while we were at the lunch table, four-year-old Quinn asked me about John, whom everyone now realized was my husband. I told him that John helps design airplane engines, but he likes to draw and paint pictures, too. Quinn was amazed that someone would do something besides design airplane engines, so I continued and told him that John also plays the harmonica. Quinn said, "You mean

John is a drawer-painter-airplane man-harmonica man?!" I said, "He sure is! He is a regular Renaissance man!"

The kids were very impressed, but immediately asked, "What's a Renaissance man?" Jessica and I knew we had our topic for the next week's lesson plan.

As usual, we took a topic and came up with definitions, history, and the parts we knew our particular children would be most interested in to start. Then depending on their interests, we could expand on activities and further topics and study the main theme of the Renaissance for as long as they wanted. In this case, it was about a month, and we focused on Leonardo da Vinci.

EMPOWERING THE CHILDREN

- Invite guest speakers to the classroom.

    ▸ In this case, John came and talked about how Leonardo's drawings were different from other artists' drawings at the time (Leonardo painted scenery behind the people, painted folds and wrinkles in the clothing, and made thousands of people wonder, "What is Mona Lisa thinking?"). John drew portraits with the kids and they drew portraits with those same details in their drawings as well.

    ▸ A student's dad who was a pilot came and showed the kids a video shot from his plane while he was flying it. Then he made paper airplanes with the kids, adding paper-clips and showing how that changed how the planes would fly.

▶▶ We continued our flying lesson through the following weeks by studying:

- How planes fly (exploring lift and drag).

- How to throw a paper airplane indoors and outdoors by looking at the technique of the world record holder.

- How to fold different types of paper airplanes. As kids became better at folding their own, they became the teachers, helping their classmates learn how to fold the planes instead of having the teachers do it.

- Illustrate and discuss the children's earliest memories after learning about Leonardo's earliest memory. His was of a bird flying over his crib, the feathers tickling his face; he always wanted to fly after that.

- Explore turtles and Leonardo's early tanks. Look at other animals and things in nature; then, invent something new!

- Learn about how the giant horse that Leonardo made out of clay was destroyed and how he chose to respond to it. (Before it could be cast in metal, a war started. Soldiers shot arrows into it and ruined it. Leonardo said he had many more projects to do, so he wasn't going to be mad about the horse.)

  ▶ Make horses out of dough or clay.

  ▶ Cover toy horses in clay.

  ▶ Discuss what you would do if someone destroyed your project.

- Learn about perspective, about how things look different depending on where you are standing.

  ‣ Draw on paper taped under the table.

  ‣ Draw items on a table while standing and then while sitting at the table. Compare and contrast the drawings.

  ‣ Draw an outdoor scene while sitting at ground level and then from a higher balcony. Compare and contrast the drawings.

  ‣ Act out a scene with your children observing from one side and then repeat the same thing with them observing from across the room. Do they see the same situation? Trade roles with them (acting vs. audience) and repeat.

- Compare, contrast, and make things fly (catapults, planes, air balloons, fairies, birds, unicorns, parachutes, bats, insects, etc.). Add feathers, wings, or use magic pixie dust. Use your imagination!

- Listen to music from the time period and dine by candlelight. (For candles, roll paper into a tube and tape them. Tape a paper flame to one end and place the candle on the table.)

- Draw and build a duomo or cathedral from blocks.

- Explore medical books, make your own drawings of body systems, and explore how bodies work (red water to pour through tubing in the water table).

- Talk about mirror writing. Write letters or words; then try to read them in the mirror. Older kids can try to write backwards and try to read their messages in the mirror.

- Pose people and draw them or use a posable wooden model like Leonardo designed.

- Carry notebooks outside, like Leonardo did, so kids can draw what interests them when they see it.

- Make egg paints, which were used at the time of Leonardo.

SUMMARY

The world is such a vast and interesting place; the opportunities for learning are endless! When your children are learning about the world, help build upon their enthusiasm by asking yourself a few questions first. What are they interested in? How can you take it further? Are there real items they can use? Remember, open-ended play leads to original solutions and problem-solving. Otherwise, you get scripted or limited play. Children's activities are important to them; their activities make up the moments in their lives. Let's help them make an impact today with what they are passionate about.

CELEBRATING LEARNING ABOUT THE WORLD THROUGHOUT THE YEAR

★

January: International Brain Teaser Month

International Creativity Month

National Poverty in America
Awareness Month

Kid Inventors' Day (17)

Bubble Wrap Appreciation Day (28)

February: Library Lovers' Month

Bubble Gum Day (1)

Groundhog Day (2)

Read in the Bathtub Day (9)

Chinese New Year/Lunar New Year (10)

March: Expanding Girls' Horizons in Science
and Engineering Month

International Ideas Month

National Umbrella Month

Youth Art Month

Fun Facts About Names Day (4)

Brain Awareness Week (Mid-month)

National Wildlife Week (Third week)

World Folk Tales and Fables
Week (Varies)

International World Day for Water (22)

April: Tsunami Awareness Month

Earth Month

World Habitat Awareness Month

National Kite Month

Sky Awareness Week (Varies)

Earth Day (22)

National Arbor Day (26)

National Go Birding Day (27)

May: Gifts from the Garden Month

National Clean Energy Month

National Inventors' Month

National Pet Month

National Transportation Week
(Mid-month)

Children's Book Week (Mid-month)

Bike-to-Work Day (17)

World Biodiversity Day (22)

National Hurricane Awareness
Week (Last week)

June: Great Outdoors Month

June Is Perennial Gardening Month

National Rivers Month

International Clothesline Week
(First week)

National Trails Day (1)

World Environment Day (5)

World Oceans Day (8)

Global Wind Day (15)

World Day to Combat Desertification
and Drought (17)

Celebration of the Senses (24)

July: National Make a Difference to
Children Month

National Recreation and Parks Month

World Population Day (11)

Take Your Houseplants for a Walk
Day (27)

Aunties Day (28)

Parents' Day (28)

August: Inventors' Month

National Water Quality Month

American Adventures Month

Happiness Happens Month

Assistance Dog Week (Beginning first Sunday)

Happiness Happens Day (8)

National Garage Sale Day (10)

International Left-Handers Day (13)

National Aviation Week (Week of the 19th)

Serendipity Day (18)

National Aviation Day (19)

September: National Wilderness Month

International Day for the Preservation of the Ozone Layer (16)

Clean Up the World Weekend (Third weekend)

World Water Monitoring Day (18)

Zero Emissions Day (21)

Car Free Day (22)

World Rivers Day (29)

October: Celebrating the Bilingual Child Month

Global Diversity Awareness Month

National Go on a Field Trip Month

Squirrel Awareness Month

National Diversity Day (4)

World Animal Day (4)

World Space Week (4-10)

Fall Astronomy Week (Varies)

World Habitat Day (7)

International Day for Natural Disaster Reduction (9)

World Planting Day (22)

International Day of Climate Action (24)

National Cat Day (29)

November: Aviation Month

National Adoption Month

National American Indian Heritage Month

Election Day (6)

America Recycles Day (15)

Celebrate Your Unique Talent Day (24)

December: World Soil Day (5)

International Mountain Day (11)

Wright Brothers' Day (17)

Chapter Seven

Respect

★

The truest form of love is how you behave toward someone, not how you feel about them.
– Steve Hall

When I was growing up, I always thought respect was something you were expected to give to your parents, to people older than you, and to people in positions of authority (teachers, police, priests, bosses, presidents, etc.). You gave them respect simply because of their positions. But I wondered whether obeying their authority without question was always the best decision. What if their words and their actions did not match?

We were expected to treat other people kindly with our words and actions—including siblings, though I had my share of typical sibling squabbles. "Other people" also referred to friends as well as acquaintances and strangers. Respect other people.

In my young mind, however, I did not realize what respect really meant. I often wondered whether it meant I should let other people get their way. If a friend wanted to play with Barbies and I wanted to draw, I would go along with what she wanted. Not a big deal. When I got to a door at the same time as someone else, I'd let the other person go first. That is having good manners, right? Later, when someone told me to give up my other friends and only be friends with her, I struggled to decide whether I was being mean to her if I said no. When I was offered a ride in a car as a young girl by a strange man, I actually felt bad for saying no and reassured him it was only because "I live right here." My problem was that I never really understood self-respect. I didn't know that I could stand up for myself as a young girl and still respect other people.

I also learned that it was important to respect property—that of my family, friends, school, and the larger community. I was expected to take care of my toys and clothing, and to take care of our furniture (no jumping on the sofa!) and house (clean up my messes). I remember seeing a TV commercial with an Indian crying because people littered the land, which opened my eyes to respecting nature as well.

Respect is something that people want for themselves, but they are often unsure how to get it. Parents and teachers expect children to be respectful, but what is often missing is treating children with respect, just for being whom they are: a member of their family, their country, humankind. This respect doesn't mean we should defer to children, but we call them by their names, treat them without prejudice, ask them thought-provoking questions, and provide answers for them when needed. In the words of R.G. Risch, "Respect is a two-way street, if you want to get it, you've got to give it." Respect that is given from mutual respect is better than respect given from deference or given out of fear of punishment or humiliation.

We can also take this idea of mutual respect even further by recognizing the self-fulfilling prophecy that comes with giving and receiving respect. Thomas S. Monson said, "When we treat people merely as they are, they will remain as they are. When we treat them as if they were what they should be, they will become what they should be." This path toward developing success is the one we want our children to follow!

> The only justification for ever looking down on
> somebody is to pick them up.
> – Jesse Jackson

SAYING NO CAN BE POSITIVE!

We have all been party to a child *begging* for a special treat or favor that we know we should say *no* to but the *begging* becomes so LOUD and insistent, often with others watching our every move, that we think, "Wouldn't it be quicker and easier to say 'Yes' *just this once? Please* let this moment end and allow some peace to return to my busy life! It won't really matter; after all, *it is just a candy bar* (Lego toy, new pair of jeans, etc.)." We have all been there as parents, as teachers, or both. Isn't it okay to give in to these little things that all children ask for?

I was fortunate to attend a lecture by David Walsh, Ph.D., the author of *No: Why Kids of All Ages Need to Hear It and Ways Parents Can Say It*. I was intrigued by this title, and as an Early Childhood Education teacher, I knew this topic was ripe for exploring in my own classroom.

I wondered: Is the goal to tell children *no*? Actually, the real goal is to teach children to say no to themselves. This makes a lot of sense. Let's think about it: Should I take an item I want even though my friend is using it? Should I eat the candy bar because I see it and it tastes good? Should I get a new toy or piece of clothing every time I go to the store? These questions could be asked by a two year old as easily as by a forty year old. Obviously, some long-term merit exists in this way of thinking. And, as far as young children are concerned, self-discipline is twice as strong a predictor of academic success as intelligence.

Walter Mischel's Marshmallow Experiment[1] (1972, Stanford) was instrumental in demonstrating this point. Mischel offered four-year-old kids one large marshmallow, which the children could eat, or they could wait fifteen minutes to receive a second marshmallow. If they ate the first marshmallow without waiting, they would not receive a second one. Researchers say children who were successful at showing the ability to delay gratification at age four were happier, had an easier time learning to read, were more successful in school, and had fewer behavioral problems at age twelve. By age eighteen, they were more likely to attend college and to graduate by age twenty-five. Correlations be-

---

1 See Dr. Walsh duplicate this study at http://www.youtube.com/watch?v=amsqeYOk--w Accessed December 13, 2012.

tween positive outcomes and the ability to say *no* to oneself have been found even up until today—thirty years after the Marshmallow Experiment. Amazing!

However, it is important to keep in mind that children who do go ahead and eat the marshmallows can still learn the skills necessary to help them learn to say *no* to themselves.

So what are the benefits of saying *no* to our children? As I mentioned, it is the foundation for self-discipline. Other benefits include respect for self and others and the development of integrity, perseverance, and high character values. Researchers have also noted high academic achievement and the corresponding economic success that usually follows.

These benefits sound great! But have you noticed that it can very difficult to say *no* in today's world? We are living in a "yes culture" where the message can generally be summed up as "more, easy, fast, and fun." Many children feel entitled; they do not realize that being born on third base isn't the same as hitting a triple, as Dr. Walsh says.

Because of this "Culture of Yes," Dr. Walsh has defined a new disorder affecting our young population that he dubs Discipline Deficit Disorder. The symptoms include:

- Distracted

- Impatient

- Culture of disrespect

- Unable to delay gratification

- Unrealistic expectations

- Entitled

- Self-centered

I imagine we have all come across children of all ages with this unofficial diagnosis!

How is this disorder related to saying *no* to your child? The brain grows in certain predictable ways. Certain windows of opportunity during childhood are more suitable for a child to accomplish specific tasks and understand specific messages. For instance, it is much easier for the brain of a two year old to learn the meaning of *no* than it is for the brain of a four year old, and so on. It does not mean that older children (and adults!) can't learn to say *no* to themselves, but it will be a much more difficult and unhappy journey for them.

Before we continue further, we need to have a frank discussion about self-esteem and how it comes into play in this whole scenario. Self-esteem is simply the opinion we have of ourselves, based on reality, including our positive and negative qualities. Unfortunately, over the years, the spread of misinformation about self-esteem has led to unhelpful child rearing practices by parents and teachers alike. A few of those myths include:

- Self-esteem comes first, and then a person becomes successful.

- Self-esteem equals feeling good.

- Stress, challenge, and disappointment damage self-esteem.

All of these are untrue. What is true is that self-esteem is like a muscle that needs to be built, leading to resilient children. After a setback, resilient children pick themselves up, dust themselves off, and try again. Resilient children know that effort is the key to their own success; that it is not based on a character trait such as being "smart." In fact, experiencing failure can be the key to future success.

How does a parent or teacher help children become resilient? You accomplish it by:

- Having a close and personal connection to them.

- Supporting them when they need it.

- Having high expectations for them.

- Showing compassion to those in need.

- Demonstrating autonomy.

- Teaching and expecting your children to be independent and resourceful.

- Being optimistic about what the future holds.

- Demonstrating flexibility and patience when required.

- Allowing yourself and children to experience the consequences of a poor choice.

Do I wait for my children to have their second birthday to begin saying *no*? No! You can begin with infants anytime they do something that for safety reasons needs to be pointed out. Gently and firmly tell your six month old that you want her to lie still on the changing table so she doesn't fall off. Tell your eight month old that your glasses stay on your face. Tell your child that it hurts when he pulls your hair by saying something like, "No pulling Mommy's hair! Ouch! It hurts Mommy."

When do children learn to do something purposefully? Researchers have determined the answer to be around fourteen to twenty months. A very interesting experiment was done using broccoli vs. goldfish crackers to help determine when children become aware that others may have different opinions about things than they do. Researchers asked toddlers to feed them a yummy treat as defined by the researcher ("I like broccoli. Yum! I don't like yucky goldfish!"). The toddler also got to feed himself a treat (toddlers tend to choose those goldfish!). If the toddler fed the researcher what the researcher liked, it was possible to tell that the child saw himself as having a different perspective than others. If the toddler only fed the researcher what she herself liked, she hadn't grasped the concept yet.

Regardless, certain behaviors should be corrected at any age, certainly by age two and up, including:

- Throwing food.
- Teasing pets.
- Aggression toward parents and siblings (this includes other adults and children, too!).
- Doing dangerous or forbidden things.

But aren't some of these behaviors normal for young children? Yes, but *normal does not mean acceptable*. It is our responsibility as caring adults to make clear what are acceptable behaviors to our youngest learners now, at the time when their brains are most open and ready to learn.

It is equally important to reinforce those qualities we want to see repeated—qualities such as politeness, respect, caring, sharing, thoughtfulness, and independence. We reinforce these qualities by noticing good manners and using them ourselves. We do it by noticing when a child puts on his coat without being asked, or when she offers a hug to a crying friend. We praise the child for all these positive behaviors that we want to encourage.

EMPOWERING THE CHILDREN

Now that we have all the background information, how do we put it into practice? Here are some simple guidelines that Dr. Walsh adheres to:

- Set limits ahead of time. Tell your child what will happen, what you expect from her, and the consequences if she chooses not to follow the rules. An example would be, "We are going to the store. You can help put items in the cart that are on the shopping list. We will not be buying candy or toys today. If you cry for candy or a toy, I will still say no."

- When you make a rule, enforce it. Remember, if it is important enough to have a rule or limit, it is important enough to follow through. For example, "If you cry or yell, I won't let you put anything else in the cart for me."

- Let children know the consequence if they cross the limit or break the rule.

- Enforce the consequence.

- Let children know they can't always get what they want.

- Support, don't rescue. Remind them that it is okay to make mistakes. Mistakes are one valuable way that all people learn.

- Encourage, don't coddle. Encouragement is better than praise, but when you do use praise, focus on effort, not ability. For example, "You worked for fifteen minutes on that puzzle and you didn't give up" is more effective than "You are so smart."

- Support and partner with schools and teachers. Make sure your child knows you are working as a team.

- Limit use of media, including no TV or computers in bedrooms, and no TV or videos before age two.

- Expect children to do chores around the house.

- Expect children to volunteer and help others.

The thing to remember is that those meltdown times, those pull-your-hair-out-of-your-head times, are truly when you are doing your most important parenting. This is when your message is really needed, your support needed, your clarity needed. Take advantage of these teachable moments and both you and your children will be the better for it. It may only be a candy bar today, but in a few short years, your "no" will have a more serious impact as you teach your child to say no to drugs, alcohol, and other socially relevant temptations.

WHAT BOX ARE YOU IN?

I was in kindergarten when I met a person with the same first name for the very first time. I can remember how Karen and I both wondered whose parents made a mistake and picked a name that was already taken. Such are the concerns of children growing up in a very small Midwest town circa 1971!

I quickly learned that there are many, many people in the world, many more people than there are names. I was okay with sharing my name with other Karens, and I even felt a bit of kinship with them. But it was the *other* names that were given to me that I never liked and never got used to.

By the time I went to first grade, I was already labeled "the good girl" by teachers and kids at school alike. Several even teased me for not making mistakes. Sounds like no mistakes would be a good thing, right? Now, I realize there are much worse identities to have. But being placed in a box is still being placed in a box. Being in any box is confining and feels awful.

Luckily for me, my box would disappear as I stepped on the porch of my house and joined my five siblings, parents, and a random cat or hamster. I was just a middle child, one of four girls and two boys in the bunch.

My box was a lonely and stressful place to be. I was born loving to learn, and I wanted to be like my older brother and sisters, so I did well in school. But I also learned that other kids sometimes got mad at the kids who got good grades, and I found that they sometimes resented me. Lots of kids assumed if you liked school, you were no fun to be around. We've all heard the saying, "All work and no play makes Jack a dull boy." But learning was important to me, so I kept studying and learning.

If some kids found out I missed a question on a test, they would tease me. That was perhaps the worst because I became so afraid of making a mistake that I would equate any potential mistake with doom and failure. Even when I did very well on a test, I was always afraid that I probably failed. Not a fun way for a kid to live!

I was great at pretending everything was fine while bottling it all up. I began making plans for my escape from my box as early as eighth grade: I already fantasized about attending the University of Illinois! College would be so fantastic. I could learn. I could be known to the University by my social security number. I would be one of thousands and thousands of nameless, faceless students. No one, besides me, would know or care what grades I got. And I would finally be Karen again.

While my experience at the University of Illinois provided me with everything I hoped for and more, I remained an overachiever. I continued to carry the fear of failure with me, but the burden became lighter as I changed my reasons for wanting to succeed. I wanted to learn to enrich myself, so I could apply the information I learned when I became a professional educator. I cared less about what the actual grades were and what they might mean to other people, although I continued to excel. To an outsider I looked no different, but on the inside I was more free.

Maybe your box was different from mine. Maybe you felt labeled because of your looks, athletic abilities, humor, or role in your family. To different people, a label may seem like a compliment, a curse, or somewhere in between. We all have our boxes from childhood. But it is important not to label our children in a way that limits them or causes undue duress. We want our children to strive to overcome their challenges and fulfill their destinies!

EMPOWERING THE CHILDREN

What can you do to avoid putting your children in a box, to avoid labeling them? Conversely, what can you do to help your children climb out of a box they may have been placed in or inadvertently crawled into themselves?

- Tell your children that they are valuable just as they are, with all their strengths and weaknesses. Let them know that qualities are changeable, based on their behaviors and experiences.

  ▸ Tell kids stories about when things were easy and when things were difficult for you. How did you cope with these situations? How did you learn? What did you learn? Children love to learn about their parents' (older siblings', relatives', teachers', etc.) lives, and sharing these stories can be a way to strengthen your relationship.

  ▸ Ask your kids what qualities they want to develop. Ice skating? Skate together or sign up for lessons. Saying no to aggressive friends? Practice different situations together, letting your children know that just like with learning to become a better basketball player, they can learn to speak more assertively and still keep their friends.

  ▸ Tell your children that people learn in different ways (some of us are visual learners, auditory learners, or tactile learners) and at different speeds. Find out what helps your children learn best and support the environment that supports them. For example, if they need quiet space to do homework and your house is noisy like most of ours, turn off the family TV and stereo during homework time. This simple act shows respect for learning styles and builds camaraderie.

- Sort toys by more than one attribute. Example: Sort toy cars by color, size, model, or number of doors. Lesson learned: People are defined by more than one aspect of themselves.

- Teach children how to consider more than one point of view. Show different perspectives in the same story by reading different versions of a familiar tale (Jon Scieszka's *The True Story of the Three Little Pigs* for the wolf's version of *The Three Little Pigs*, for example). Discuss and change sides when role playing a scenario to see what the other side feels like. Act out different characters in a play.

- Have a "no exclusion" policy of participation, meaning we must not exclude someone because of whom he or she is. However, it is an appropriate sanction to say, "I don't want to play with you because you ripped my drawing (hit me, called me a name, etc.)."

- Encourage cooperation by putting diverse groups together to work toward a common goal. For little guys, it could be finding all of the red items in the room and collecting them in a box, sharing the easel for partner art, carrying a large item across the room or playground together, etc.

- It is also important to teach the positive and negative associations with colors and characters of color.

  ▸ For example, the color blue is associated with calm, cold, and feeling sad.

  ▸ Be sure to use the colors brown and black as beautiful decorations and not refer to them as "ugly" colors.

  ▸ Represent heroes in the classroom or home (using dolls, books, posters, etc.) with people or characters from the same cultural background as your children as well as those from the cultures of the "friends we have not met yet." This activity also helps to ease the fears many children have when joining a new school, beginning a new activity like dance class, or even playing at the park where they may not know anyone else. Strangers can then be considered as potential new friends instead of people to be feared.

- Be respectful and call people by their given names. If you've given your children nicknames or pet names, ask their permission to use them in public once they are older or show sensitivity to it. Ask your children to have the same consideration for other people.

- Provide children who need help asserting themselves with words they can say. For example, "All people make mistakes. That's how we learn." Practice different situations with your children in order to build their confidence.

When we treat people respectfully, as the unique individuals that they are, they tend to treat us with respect in return. This is the path to greater understanding not only of others but of ourselves. Only then can we have the opportunity to reach our true potentials.

The earth does not belong to us. We belong to the earth.
– Chief Seattle, The Chief Seattle's Speech

RESPECT FOR NATURE

One thing I have found from year after year of being with young children is that most of them absolutely love animals. They will point to birds as older infants, and once their bodies are capable, will crawl, walk, chase, and climb to reach cats, dogs, squirrels, bugs, and other creatures they happen to see. Along with our "Safety first" rule for kids ("It's not okay to chase the animals into the street!"), we need to teach a respect for the bodies of the animals and their environment as well. A great starting point is capitalizing on children's love for animals.

One year, Jessica and I had a particular group of children who were extremely animal-oriented. Not a day went by that at least half of them were not pretending to be animals at any given time. Cats would be meowing for us to give them a treat of a mouse or a fish from our pockets, owners would be attaching chains to their dogs and walking them around the room, birds would be flying throughout the classroom.

Luckily for me, I was able to attend a wonderful training by representatives of the Wilderness Awareness School in Duvall, Washington. I highly recommend their book *Coyote's Guide to Connecting with Nature* by Jon Young,

Evan McGown, and Ellen Haas. The approach of Coyote mentoring relies on teachers reintroducing children to nature through play and joy in the "invisible school...having direct experience with plants and animals just beyond the edge of their back yards."

Because we learn skills through brain patterning, our brain is able to make a neurological shortcut so we can learn new skills without thinking if we repeat an activity. With our modern lives, without consciously learning some "core routines of nature connection," we may miss out on nature's sensory input and even be unaware of its presence in our everyday world.

Storytelling to capture the imagination is also a key component used to connect with children. Stories can be personal in nature (and are very powerful because they are true and happened to you!), animal feats, or traditional tales from different cultures. These types of stories can easily create a powerful and emotional response from the children. Imagine how interesting and how much of an impact you could make by incorporating your discussion of the water cycle into your own story of rafting down a river!

Stories can also be memorized (some cultures require it because oral storytelling is how they transmit information from generation to generation) or improvised. In order to keep the listeners engaged, use a variety of voices, add a repeated refrain, add actions and gestures, use silent pauses for dramatic effect, and have lots of fun.

Another thing we immediately adopted in our classroom was the Wilderness Awareness School's concept of using our five senses to the fullest while in nature, just as the various animals use their five senses: owl eyes to see better in nature, deer ears to hear better in nature, raccoon hands when exploring in nature, fox feet when walking, and a super-sniffer nose for smelling. We began to tune in more while outside and to pay attention to the little things.

We also learned that if we wanted to learn about animals, we needed to learn about plants and how animals use them for food, shelter, and camouflage. We discovered that if we trampled through the outdoors, we would scare the animals away and we would destroy their homes.

The opportunity to visit a forest presented itself as part of a field trip. The children were so excited about what they might see, hear, touch, and smell while on this trip. The kids wondered, "Wouldn't it be fun to be a tree in the forest and experience everything that happens in the forest?" Jessica and I thought, "Why not be a forest of trees walking quietly through the forest?"

So we painted our faces so we would blend into the forest. We gathered sticks, flowers, and leaves to attach to headbands for our heads. We practiced walking with fox feet so we wouldn't scare animals away. We used egg timers to see how long we could quietly stand still while we were outside. If we were lucky, maybe a squirrel or a bird would think we were real trees!

Although on the day of the field trip, no actual animals thought we were trees, we saw lots of grown-ups on the bus, and we were happy to spread the message to take care of animals and plants in nature or they will go live somewhere else or perish.

EMPOWERING THE CHILDREN

- To help children of all ages connect with nature through direct exploration, stories, and games, I highly recommend the book *Coyote's Guide to Connecting with Nature* by Jon Young, Evan McGown, and Ellen Haas.

- Introduce the concept of using our five senses to the fullest while in nature, just as the various animals use their five senses:

  ▶ Owl eyes to see better in nature.

    ▶▶ Hide objects in a room, gradually using smaller ones, to challenge visual senses. For example, begin with larger stuffed animals and work down to smaller animal figurines.

    ▶▶ Repeat this same activity outdoors.

    ▶▶ Have children choose an apple and really look at it. Put all apples in a bowl; then have each child try to find his or her apple. You can also do this activity with rocks, leaves, etc.

    ▶▶ Take photos of children's hands or feet. Have children identify each other by photos.

  ▶ Deer ears to hear better in nature.

    ▶▶ Have one child close his eyes and turn to face away from the group. Point to another child, having that child say, "Hello." The child with eyes closed must identify the other child by voice only.

▸▸ Use Coyote's book to learn about the different types of bird calls. Identity call types while outside (hunger, keeping in touch, danger).

▸ Raccoon hands when exploring in nature.

- Put a variety of objects in a bag; reach in the bag without looking and identify them by touch.

- Blindfold a child; have the child hold a friend's hand and identify the person by touch. No talking!

▸ Fox feet when walking.

▸▸ Walk silently on grass, wood chips, gravel, dirt.

▸▸ Play the game "The Animals Are Watching." Have the children who want to be animals quietly hide in the trees, bushes, etc. The other kids walk through the area trying to count all of the animals they see.

▸ Super-sniffer nose for smelling.

▸▸ Tape strips of paper on the floor, creating an intersecting pathway. Put peppermint or orange extract on one path, lavender essential oil on another. While on their hands and knees, can the children follow and identify the paths by scent, even when they intersect?

- Have a "sit spot" or place in nature for your kids to return to often in order to learn to sit still, increase attention span, be alone, and notice nature. It can be a special spot in your yard, on your porch, or be a spot in a park. Your children may have a great spot you've never considered (perhaps outside the back door where spiders make webs or a spot on the sidewalk out front).

- Stay on paths when hiking.

- Pick up litter and use the trash/recycle/compost containers provided.

- Do not feed the wildlife.

- Explore maps. Kids love to look at them and draw their own. You can pick up free maps at the airport or local visitors bureaus.

- Take local bird guides, plant guides, and animal guides with you when you take your children to the park, lake, or even for a walk in the city. What can you identify? Pay attention and mark your discoveries. You may be very surprised by what is living under your noses!

- It is also crucial to tap into childhood passions in order to connect nature with children. What are these types of activities?

  ▸ Ones that get our adrenaline pumping, such as jumping, leaping, and running.

  ▸ Hiding, seeking, and sneaking through trees, around rocks, and under bushes.

  ▸ Hunts, errands (collecting kindling for the fireplace, picking up litter), and adventures (spotting owls).

  ▸ Pretend adventures, such as treasure hunting or animal tracking.

OIL SPILLS

When the Deepwater Horizon oil spill occurred off the coast of Louisiana on April 20, 2011, the news was all over the TV and newspapers. It is back in the news again as BP learns of the fines it must pay for its part in this tragedy. Today, children may have questions about this or other oil spills.

The kids in my classroom last year couldn't help but learn about this catastrophe since it dominated the news. One way they expressed their knowledge and concern was through their artwork.

One morning in May 2011, I put rainbow scratch paper (black paper with rainbow colors underneath it that is revealed when scratched with a wooden tool) on the table in the art area. I told the children that they could make anything they wanted to make with it. This activity was open-ended for the purpose of free expression and fine motor practice.

While I was aware of the oil spill, I was surprised that the children were so aware of it. David made what appeared to be an oval shape and filled most of it in. He told me, "It's an oil spill." I wrote his name and title on it; then I asked him what he knew about oil spills. He said, "They're bad to the earth and the animals. It exploded." After a bit more discussion, he revealed that the oval "Stops the oil from going all over the world." He had drawn a containment boom around his oil spill.

Emile also made an oil spill and repeated that "They are bad." Sabrina and Annisa agreed. Annisa called her drawing "Mixed-Up Oil Spill/Tricky Oil Spill." Sabrina referred to hers as "Ariel in the Oil Spill." Tommy also made an "Oil Spill," but he did not seem to know what an oil spill was. As you can see, each child put the oil spill into a context that was relatable to him or her. It was linked to something negative, confusing, or unknown, and a swimming Disney princess.

Since children began to ask questions about the oil spill, it seemed fitting to discuss it in our classroom to cement some of the issues in their minds. A few children brought in newspaper clippings and we talked about them during our Morning Meeting. We realized we should do some experiments of our own to learn more about oil spills, especially since children learn by doing. We put clear water in large tubs and added feathers, toy birds, and fish. Next, we made an oil spill in our water by adding cooking oil and black food coloring to see what would happen to the feathers and the animals.

As you can imagine, lots of discussion followed. As a teacher, I really enjoy when young children show an interest in current events and I can help them learn to problem solve, coming up with ideas for how they might make a difference in the world. Continue reading for ideas to spur your own children's exploration.

EMPOWERING THE CHILDREN

Following are examples of how you can explore a disaster such as an oil spill with children. But please use it as a guideline and modify it to meet your needs for other topics:

- Discuss more in depth with the children about oil spills:
  - ▸ What is oil?
  - ▸ Where does it come from?
  - ▸ How is it made?
  - ▸ Why do people drill for it?
  - ▸ Why do they drill in the ocean?
  - ▸ How is oil used?
  - ▸ What occurs when there is a spill, including the effect on the environment, the effect on animals, the possible effects for the future, etc.?
  - ▸ Why are companies given fines for making poor decisions?
  - ▸ Are there alternatives to using oil?
- Make a water and oil slick in the sensory table.
  - ▸ How is the water different?
    - ▸▸ Would you want to drink it?
    - ▸▸ Would you want to swim in it?
  - ▸ Add feathers.
    - ▸▸ Have the children compare the feathers before and after being in the water.
    - ▸▸ What happens after the feathers dry?
    - ▸▸ Do they feel different?
    - ▸▸ Are they different weights?
    - ▸▸ Can you make the feathers feel "okay" again?

- ‣‣ If you were a bird, how would you fly if you had oil on your wings?
- ‣ Add toy animals to the oily water.
  - ‣‣ How can you make the toys feel "okay" again?
  - ‣‣ If you were a fish, how would you breathe if you had oil on your gills?
- ‣ Wash the feathers and toys with dish soap.
  - ‣‣ What happens?
- Discuss our relationship with the earth.
  - ‣ The gifts we get from the earth:
    - ‣‣ Homes for people, animals, and plants
    - ‣‣ Air
    - ‣‣ Water
    - ‣‣ Food
    - ‣‣ Natural resources such as oil, etc.
  - ‣ What the earth needs from us:
    - ‣‣ To understand it
    - ‣‣ Take care of it
    - ‣‣ Speak for it
  - ‣ How to be a friend to the earth:
    - ‣‣ Reduce, reuse, and recycle
  - ‣ How to be a voice for the earth:
    - ‣‣ Teach others how to take care of the earth since trees, flowers, animals, soil, air, and water can't talk!

Although oil spills may seem like a topic above the comprehension or interest of preschoolers, you will be surprised at their understanding of tragedies such as these and their compassion for the people, animals, and natural habitats in our world. I recently talked to a father whose son was in my classroom at that time, and his son still keeps track of oil spills in the news a year and a half later. Let's believe in our young people today!

REDUCE, REUSE, RECYCLE

The classroom's art area was open for exploration for most of the morning. In addition to the planned project of making snakes from paper plates for our rain forest, the children were free to create whatever they liked using the materials that interested them.

Caitlin had been drawing and cutting for about half an hour. She noticed she had two small pieces of paper left, each roughly the size of her hand. She asked me to help trace her hand with a marker since the paper was "too small to hold on to." After I traced her hand, she returned to the art area and I went on my fifteen-minute break. When I returned, Caitlin ran up to me and excitedly showed me her "gloves." She had placed the paper with the traced hand on top of the other paper and cut out the hand, making two hand cut-outs at once. She then taped the pieces together, around her left hand, making a glove.

Angie came to the art area and had the choice of using large pieces of paper or some smaller scraps of paper for her project. She said, "I want to make a card for my mom."

She chose one of the smaller pieces of paper and drew her picture.

Sabrina made a snake from a paper plate and cut part of the plate off. She said to the other children at the table, "Who wants to use this scrap?" None of the other children wanted to use it so Sabrina said, "Maybe someone can take it home to use it later." She finished her snake and left the art area.

Annisa was drawing on one side of a piece of paper. After she finished drawing her picture, she turned her paper over and drew on the other side of the paper.

Emile made a representation of himself with a scared face like when he sees a spider. He drew his face on a smaller piece of paper plate, taped that to a paper body, and then added paper legs. When he asked me how to make arms, I told him to look around to see whether he saw anything that gave him an idea how to do it. He saw the paper plate scraps that earlier Sabrina had tried to give away and said, "I know! I can use these for arms!" He taped them to his project and admired his work.

Caitlin also found one tiny piece of pink paper that she wrapped around her thumb; then she taped the ends together. Now she had a thumb ring!

I looked inside the paper recycling bin, which typically had been full of lots of usable scrap paper, and saw only a tiny bit of small scraps were left in it.

Why are these events worth mentioning? Because they took place two weeks after the kids had learned about the Deepwater Horizon oil spill and we began discussing the importance of taking care of the earth. Because the children studied the effects of oil spills (such as the one in Louisiana) on animals, humans, and the environment, and they had learned about reducing, reusing, recycling, and how to be an advocate for the planet, it was interesting for me to observe some of the children a few weeks later to see what, if any, changes they had made in their behavior.

I had been on vacation for two weeks, so I really wasn't sure what I would observe since I had not been at school to remind them about what they could do to reduce or reuse in the classroom. I was very pleased to see that they were spontaneously making the decision to use small pieces of paper when they were going to cut the paper into little pieces anyway or did not need the whole piece of paper. Past behavior showed a clear preference for new unblemished sheets of paper. Jessica and I never saw the children use both sides of the paper before our unit on being a friend to the earth. We often had to pull pieces of paper out of the recycling bin that had small tears or cuts out of them and tell the children that those pieces were still good pieces of paper that could be used. Last year we had a scrap paper bin, but no one wanted to use the paper placed in it. This group seems to have really made the connection, and hopefully, they are learning some great lifelong habits.

EMPOWERING THE CHILDREN

- Add a scrap bin to your home or classroom. Ask the children to look in the bin first for paper before cutting big pieces of paper.

- Comment to the kids when you notice that they are using materials creatively and not wasting them.

- Make more projects out of recycled materials (planters out of yogurt containers, piggy banks out of plastic bottles, rain sticks out of paper towel rolls, etc.).

- Make the topic of being a friend to the earth a frequent one, so the children really learn to consider their actions and the effects they may have on other people, the environment, and animals.

SUMMARY

Respect is a far-reaching concept. It applies to respecting parents, persons in authority, friends, strangers, and ourselves. It applies to our environment and the animals and plants that inhabit it because we need a healthy ecosystem for our children to live in. It applies to personal property and even ideas. By being good role models, explaining what respect means, and providing the answers children need to understand *why* they should be respectful, our children will be well on their way to success today and tomorrow.

CELEBRATING RESPECT THROUGHOUT THE YEAR

★

January:	Be Kind to Food Servers Month
	Celebration of Life Month
	International Child-Centered Divorce Month
	Self-Love Month
	World Religion Day (20)
February:	International Boost Self-Esteem Month
	International Expect Success Month
	National Time Management Month
	Plant the Seeds of Greatness Month
	Return Shopping Carts to the Supermarket Month
	Inconvenience Yourself Day (27)
March:	International Ideas Month
	Listening Awareness Month
	National Ethics Awareness Month
	Celebrate Your Name Week (First week)
	Namesake Day (3)
	International Day for the Elimination of Racial Discrimination (21)

	National Week of the Ocean (March 31-April 6)
April:	Month of the Young Child
	National Donate Life Month
	Weed Out Hate: Sow the Seeds of Peace Day (3)
	National Love Our Children Day (6)
	National Siblings Day (10)
	Consumer Awareness Week (varies)
	National Park Week (varies)
	Kindergarten Day (21)
	Spank Out Day USA (30)
May:	International Civility Awareness Month
	Be Kind to Animals Week (varies)
	Native American Rights Recognized May 12, 1879
	Work at Home Moms Week (varies)
	National Etiquette Week (Second Monday)
	International Day of United Nations Peacekeepers (29)
June:	Children's Awareness Month
	Effective Communications Month

Say Something Nice Day (1)

Multicultural American Child Awareness Day (9)

Work @ Home Father's Day (Friday before Father's Day)

America's Kids Day (23)

July: Cell Phone Courtesy Month

National Make a Difference to Children Month

Made in the USA Day (2)

Compliment Your Mirror Day (3)

Tell the Truth Day (7)

Toss Away the "Could Haves" and "Should Haves" Day (20)

August: Get Ready for Kindergarten Month

National Win with Civility Month

Respect for Parents Day (1)

September: International People Skills Month

National Courtesy Month

National Grandparents Day (First Sunday after Labor Day)

Emancipation Proclamation (22)

October: Global Diversity Awareness Month

	National Bullying Prevention and Awareness Month
	World Teachers' Day (5)
November:	National Inspirational Role Models Month
	National Parents as Teachers Day (8)
	World Kindness Day (13)
	Universal Children's Day (20)
December:	International Day of Persons with Disabilities (3)
	Human Rights Week (Week of the 10th)
	Underdog Day (20)

Chapter Eight

Responsibility

★

If you want children to keep their feet on the
ground, put some responsibility on their shoulders.
– Abigail Van Buren

When discussing responsibility and children, we are really talking about two different things: our responsibility as adults *to the children* to protect and provide for them, and the responsibility that children *must develop within themselves*. To begin, I think it is important to discuss the overall vision we have of the world because our vision colors how we act in our daily lives, which in turn affects how children act in theirs by playing off our moods and by imitating our actions.

I really am a believer. I believe that we will arrive at a time in the future where we will no longer have large wars on this planet and people will respond responsibly instead of react irrationally. Why do I believe this? Because I have looked at evidence—facts from the past and present—to see that people are changing the world for the better in peaceable ways.

We see it when we look at the abolition of slavery, the Civil Rights Movement, and the Woman's Rights movement. More and more adults around the world are standing up for those who are different from themselves and taking responsibility for our collective futures.

But we also need to look more specifically at children because we have all seen kids bite and hit each other, and we probably even did a little bit of this ourselves as we were growing up. Lots of children like to pretend to shoot each other with toy or imaginary guns, too. Does that mean kids are born violent and we just have to civilize them first?

CHILDREN AND ROUGH-HOUSING

Some people argue that since children enjoy wrestling and play-fighting, they must be violent by nature. This theory ignores the fact that both humans and animals like to engage in activities such as wrestling when it is not violent in order to gain physical and social benefits. These benefits are related to new neuron growth in the brain that results from the physical activity that wrestling provides. This neuron growth enhances balance and coordination skills, improves muscle strength, and builds stronger social bonds. This activity, again, is true in humans and animals (puppies, bears, and everything in between).

If you were to observe closely the different postures and facial expressions in both children and animals when they are playing vs. when they are fighting in an aggressive manner, you would be able to see clear differences. During pretend play or in its natural state, once one of the players experiences pain or injury, or when it is no longer a playful and fun game, the parties stop the activity and retreat from the wrestling. Since animals of the same species do not try to kill each other, this may look like one bear walking away when it has made the point that he is stronger. The animal does not take actions further than it needs to in order to get its message across. Likewise, animals with horns or antlers "wrestle" each other only against their horns or antlers, and save using their horns or antlers to maim or kill an enemy by striking in the enemy's soft and vulnerable body parts.

During the normal course of play for children, once a look of fear crosses the face of one or the laughter stops, the kids naturally back off from each other, realizing the play has gone too far. A simple shout to stop or a cry of pain does the job as well. So why do so many teachers (or even parents) ban this kind of physical play when kids can benefit from it, improving neuron growth, social bonds, and learning that responsible line of "do not cross this"? Do we really believe kids to be naturally violent?

Most likely not. Usually it has to do with the inappropriate physical space and amount of supervision that can be properly provided in a group of fifteen to twenty preschoolers and up to thirty-five kindergarteners. Teachers can do children a favor by telling them *why* the rules are in place. I know it helped the preschoolers in my care to explain the word "roughhouse" to them; it has the word "house" in it, so it is safest to do at home under the supervision of parents. Most families have a more manageable number of children so supervision is easier. Otherwise we would call it "rough-schooling!" This explanation made sense to the children. But whenever possible, Jessica and I allowed them to use their whole bodies (rolling down the hills at the park, climbing trees, etc.) to chase each other and challenge their balance, coordination, strength, and build their friendships. Parents can do this as well.

Children need to learn the physical boundaries of their bodies and how to use their bodies responsibly. They need to learn how to use their strength, their speed, their maneuverability through a variety of real experiences. Accidents may happen, but accidents also teach them how to readjust their bodies and learn responsibility for their actions. We need to trust kids to learn from their mistakes. Cuts and bumps hurt for a short time but will heal. Learning how to be more gentle and careful next time will last a lifetime. Knowing the adults in your life trust you to try new skills and provide opportunities to practice them also lasts a lifetime.

MODELING FOR CHILDREN

From quite an early age, children begin to model what they see and hear the important people in their lives do and say. Important people can be parents, siblings, friends, teachers, you name it! As I mentioned in the first paragraph of this book, I actually decided to become an Early Childhood Education professional because a toddler I occasionally babysat in high school imitated my gestures, much to my surprise!

Researchers have been studying the phenomenon of how children imitate adults since the 1960s. A famous experiment with a "Bobo" doll (an inflatable three-foot doll that looks like a clown and bounces back up every time it's knocked down) demonstrated how children learn and repeat violent acts that they observe.[1]

Not only did the researchers discover that children imitate the same behaviors that they see adults partake in, but the researchers also observed children expanding their violent repertoire to include additional forms of violence not observed. In this study, the adult punched the Bobo doll and hit it with a toy hammer. Children also began to jump on the doll and shoot it with a toy gun, even though the adult never participated in these activities.

What can we take away from this study/video? Children imitate violent acts they see as well as transfer one form of violence into other forms of violence. What else is important about the Bobo doll research? Researchers have found the results are the same whether the acts are observed in person or observed in the media (TV, video games, etc.). This evidence concludes then that negative behaviors are learned, and it goes to follow that positive ones can be learned as well.

A final point must be made. *Please remember that just because a behavior is developmentally more likely to occur at a certain age, if the behavior is inappropriate or dangerous, it must be addressed at the time and an alternative behavior given to replace it.* For example, just because many toddlers bite does not mean it is okay for your little one to bite. Tell him or her "Ouch! No biting people." Provide the child with a toy to bite instead.

---

1 The video can be viewed at http://www.youtube.com/watch?v=lCETgT_Xfzg&feature=related) Accessed December 14, 2012.

EMPOWERING THE CHILDREN

What can we do to make sure we are helping our children learn appropriate social skills? Model and tell them what you approve of, what behaviors you like. Do you want your children to take their shoes off inside the house? Take your own shoes off, tell them to take their shoes off, and don't forget to tell them why! ("It keeps the dirt off the carpet," for example.)

Here are a few more for you:

Children's Desired Behavior	Adult's Job	Why?
• Walking inside (don't run inside).	• Walk inside home, school, stores, Grandma's, etc. • Ask other caregivers to follow same rule. • May explain it like "turtle feet inside, rabbit outside." • Provide lots of outdoor time to run around.	• Safety first. • People. • Belongings.
• Volume of voice inside: Using a "talking voice."	• Use a "talking voice:" No yelling. • Practice "whisper, talk, yell."	• Respect for others. • Hurts your ears. • Wakes up baby.

	• Explain it like "red light or green light" voices. • Explain it as using a "mouse voice, lion voice." • Turn TV down or off.	
• Using gentle touches and kind words.	• Use gentle touches and kind words with self, kids, adults, pets.	• Feels good to other person. • Feels good to self. • Shows love and respect. • Others will enjoy playing with you.
• Listening to you.	• Listen to your child. • Remember, listening to your child is not the same as giving in to your child! It is hearing what he or she is trying to express and considering it.	• Respect. • We take turns in our family. • Decisions are made after hearing the facts.

SUPERHERO ACADEMY

As you may have noticed, superhero toys and play are usually very popular with children. Kids express much enthusiasm and excitement with this type of play. However, some children's behavior gets a little too rambunctious and out of control with this type of play, so it is frequently banned from schools. What is a parent or teacher to do when superhero characters are so popular yet they have some redeeming values? We want to make sure we provide the children with fun and safe activities they can use to practice some of the desirable Super Power skills.

Young children are drawn to such characters for many reasons, including:

- People of all ages look up to and admire superheroes.

- Superheroes are powerful and strong.

- Superheroes can solve any problem.

- Superheroes are known to be good.

What we need to do is reinforce to the children the virtues of some of their favorite characters. For example, superheroes use their powers to help people and do not use weapons to hurt someone. Superheroes also have a lot of responsibility to use their powers to do good things, and like the police, have lots of training to be safe as they try to find a solution to a problem. We can also teach our kids about real-life superheroes by exposing them to real role models who demonstrate the virtues we all admire so much. We can also provide an opportunity for children to emulate and experience superhero abilities.

EMPOWERING THE CHILDREN

- Provide "Superhero Tips," ideas related to the healthy foods and exercise superheroes must responsibly eat and perform to remain healthy and available to help those in need.

- Discuss the responsibility of police officers to help others solve problems, and the lengthy training they go through to make sure they are safe and keep others safe. Talk about how most officers never fire their weapons in real life. Refer to Chapter 1 for more information on gun safety and gun education.

- Ask your children:

  ‣ What super power they would each like to have. Is there a way to develop that virtue in real life?

  ‣ How would you be a peacekeeper?

  ‣ What's your superhero name?

  ‣ Play "What would you do if...?" Make up different scenarios and discuss their answers, providing guidance and more questions as needed.

  ‣ Have your kids take the Superhero Pledge. Write your own to fit your needs, but consider including parts about pledging to keep my body healthy by eating fruits and vegetables, exercising, and getting enough sleep every day. Include using your skills for peace and construction, being humble, and helping to fix mistakes. You can even make badges for the kids to sign and carry.

- Make your children's favorite stuffed animal friend into "Super Teddy." Add a paper or cloth cape, mask, foil boots, and any other embellishments for a superhero costume for him/her to wear! If you are a classroom teacher, plan "Super Teddy Tuesday." Have the kids bring a favorite stuffed animal to school that is easy for them to carry around the classroom or playground. Make the costumes at school and have a parade!

- Have kids dress as their favorite superheroes! Make masks and capes to reflect specific superheroes or invent original ones.

- Discuss non-graphic newspaper articles about natural disasters. Talk about the ways people are helping other people who need it.

  ‣ Provide an aid tent (sheet over a table, for example), emergency supplies (doctor kits, water bottles, food, walkie-talkies, helmets, rope ladder, camouflage tarp, pulleys, buckets, trucks, rescue vehicles, food rations, medical supplies, boats, sand bags, helicopters), and rescue worker ID's. Other kids or toy dolls/animals can be "rescued" and cared for. Even though many adults traditionally think of a catapult as a weapon, a toy catapult can be used as a tool to launch rescue supplies (toy food, bundles of bandages, etc.) to stranded people and animals in a play situation. Cranes and ladders can add to this experience and provide a physics lesson as well.

  ‣ For an earthquake, have a pan or tub of soil. Add little people, buildings, cars. Shake it and see what happens. Rescue people.

- Practice fire, tornado, and earthquake drills.

- Have a first aid demonstration, including supplies for children to experiment with.

▶ Don't forget to include calling 911! Demonstration, permission to call, and practice on a toy phone or cell without batteries are all important.

- To encourage development of physical skills, make an obstacle course, have a mini boot camp, or have kids carry buckets of water without spilling!

When a man points a finger at someone else, he should remember that four of his fingers are pointing at himself.
– Louis Nizer

Now that we've clarified for children our expectations, how do we get them to take responsibility for their actions when things do not go as planned? Admitting our mistakes and figuring out how to make amends can be scary for people of all ages!

THE HUMMINGBIRD EGG

One sunny morning, a student brought an amazing discovery to our preschool classroom: a real hummingbird egg. The egg was so tiny, about the size of an adult's fingernail, and extremely fragile. Jessica and I discussed whether or not we should put it in a little magnifying display box. The clear cube would allow the children to see the egg and preserve it, but prevent them from actually touching it, smelling it, experiencing it fully.

As teachers and parents, we often come across items that are very valuable and unique. We want to use them, but we are almost afraid to use them. They are too special! We don't trust ourselves or others to be responsible enough with them. But how can we learn responsibility if we are never provided with truly valuable items?

Jessica and I chose to display the egg without the protective display box. We knew the egg would most likely be broken in the morning at some point, but we thought the egg represented a valuable learning opportunity for not only the children, but for us. We made a little nest for the egg and drew a picture to symbolize "No Squishing." On the table the egg went, ready for the children to see as they walked in the room.

About five minutes after we put the egg on display, Julia and her mom approached me. Julia's mom said, "Julia has something she wants to tell you."

I could tell Julia did not have something she *wanted* to tell me, but something she was *supposed* to tell me. I could tell because Julia's body was rigid and she had her eyes closed *very* tightly. She couldn't even look at me. This posture led me to assume that the hummingbird egg had been broken. I knew that how I chose to handle this situation would be important in my relationship not only with Julia, but with how Julia viewed what had happened and how she viewed herself.

I was a bit disappointed that the egg was already broken, but *I chose* to put it out so children like Julia could have the chance to explore it, and hopefully, being careful would result in an intact egg for the day. Julia was as careful as she was able to be on this day. I also remembered how I spent too much of my time being worried about making mistakes as I was growing up, and I absolutely didn't want that kind of worrying to be Julia's pattern.

So I told her that no matter what she wanted to tell me, it was okay. I loved her now and I would love her just as much after she told me what had happened. She softened up a bit and I pulled her onto my lap. Although her eyes were still closed, Julia told me she squeezed the egg too much and it broke. I told her to open her eyes and look at mine. Did they look like mad eyes? *No.* Could she see I still loved her? *Yes.* I thanked her for being brave and telling me the truth. I told her she had been responsible.

Next on the agenda: how to make amends. Julia told me she was sorry she squished the egg, and I told her I forgave her. We decided to take a photo of the squished egg so other kids could see it, and we cleaned up the mess. Julia held my hand as she told Jessica what happened; with this support, she was able to keep her eyes open. Later at morning meeting, Julia told the kids what she discovered: hummingbird eggs are more fragile than you think they will be and teachers love kids even when they make mistakes. Teachers will even show them how to fix things and feel better. I was amazed at Julia's strength and how it grew over the course of an hour or two. I hope that strength has stayed with her and that she can call upon it when she needs it.

Follow-up: Julia was in my classroom for two years and she became one of the most responsible and careful children in the room. She took a lot of pride in being a responsible person and being given more responsibility because we trusted her. She also took children who were new to the classroom under her wing to make sure they understood how to be responsible members of our classroom community.

EMPOWERING THE CHILDREN

- Listen. Breathe. Listen some more.

- Gentle touches show a warm acceptance of the person, not the behavior.

- Separate the unacceptable behavior from the person.

- Reassure kids of your acceptance and love. Help them read your body language.

- Use words such as responsibility, honesty, and courage.

- Find ways to make amends. Have the children come up with their own ideas and you can help guide them or support them in carrying them out.

- Discuss with your kids mistakes you've made and how you've handled them. They will be relieved to know they can live through tough times, just like you did.

- Role play scenarios using puppets, animals, dolls, or just yourselves. See what works, what doesn't work, and explore why. Switch roles to gain more perspective.

> **No snowflake in an avalanche ever feels responsible.**
> **– Voltaire**

CHORES

Another part of responsibility relates to chores at home or jobs at school. I'm a firm believer that children have a strong desire to be part of a group, a family, a classroom. Being part of a group provides you with a safe haven, support, interesting conversation, and opportunities to explore and learn. Being part of a group also means that we all have a responsibility to respect each other and the space we live, learn, and grow in. In addition to building responsibility, it builds the confidence and self-help skills that are necessary once your children are grown up.

EMPOWERING THE CHILDREN

- Expect all members of the family or classroom to lend a hand, and demonstrate how to accomplish the different tasks.

  - ▶ For example, even toddlers can put toys in a bin, clothes in a laundry basket, and garbage in the can. Preschoolers can put silverware on the table, sort laundry (match socks, Mom's clothes, Dad's clothes, baby clothes, by color, etc.). Day-cares and preschools are full of teachers who implement job boards where kids get to pick a job and implement it each day.

  - ▶ For children who are reluctant to clean, make it interesting. Can you pick up all of the blue Legos before I pick up the red ones? Provide children with their own cleaning tools (broom and dustpan, washcloth, etc.) that are easy for them to access without adult help to encourage independence.

  - ▶ Have clear expectations and enforce them. For example, put your toys away before pulling out the next one, before dinner, or bedtime.

  - ▶ Do not pay kids for regular expected chores. Pay includes giving them stickers and other tokens. Research has found that this practice undermines your efforts. Reward children for extras like helping to clean out the garage, for example, but not for making their beds or cleaning up their toys. That is what people who have beds or toys are expected to do. It is their responsibility to care for them.

SUMMARY

By providing children with opportunities to learn their physical boundaries through active play, we can help them to become more responsible for their physical actions. In addition, role models provide examples of acceptable ways to behave in good times and when they make mistakes. Explaining to children why specific traits make another person worth emulating is powerful. Children want to be responsible and have others model after them. Let's provide them with opportunities to rise to the occasion!

CELEBRATING RESPONSIBILITY
THROUGHOUT THE YEAR

★

January: Get Organized Month

International Child-Centered
Divorce Month

National Be On-Purpose Month

National Mentoring Month

February: Library Lovers' Month

National Bird-Feeding Month

National Children's Dental
Health Month

National Time Management Month

Relationship Wellness Month

Return Shopping Carts to the
Supermarket Month

Youth Leadership Month

March: Credit Education Month

International Listening
Awareness Month

Return the Borrowed Books Week
(First week)

Check Your Batteries Day (10)

Fill Our Staplers Day (Monday after Daylight Savings Time begins)

Organize Your Home Office Day (12)

Grass is Always Browner on the Other Side of the Fence Day (30)

April: Car Care Month

Physical Wellness Month

Stress Awareness Month

World Habitat Awareness Month

International Pooper Scooper Week (1-7)

Weed Out Hate: Sow the Seeds of Peace Day (3)

National Teach Children to Save Day (23)

Take Our Daughters and Sons to Work Day (25)

May: National Bike Month

National Babysitters Day (11)

National Etiquette Week (Second Monday)

June: Adopt-A-Shelter-Cat Month

National Hunger Awareness Month

Hunger Day (6)

	Public Service Day (23)
July:	Cell Phone Courtesy Month
	National Make a Difference to Children Month
	Tell the Truth Day (7)
August:	International Win with Civility Month
	What Will Be Your Legacy Month
September:	AKA Responsible Dog Ownership Month
	National Courtesy Month
	Library Card Sign-Up Month
	Kids Take Over the Kitchen Day (13)
October:	Adopt-A-Shelter-Dog Month
	Hunger Awareness Month
	National Bullying Prevention and Awareness Month
	National Pet Wellness Month
	Positive Attitude Month
	World Humanitarian Action Day (8)
	Drive Safely to Work Week (First week)
	National Food Bank Week (Week of the 16th)

November: Fill Our Staplers Day (Monday after
              Daylight Savings Time ends)

              General Election Day (First Tuesday
              after the first Monday)

December: Eat a Red Apple Day (1)

Chapter Nine

Courage

★

*A hero is no braver than an ordinary man, but he
is braver five minutes longer.*
– Ralph Waldo Emerson

MY FEAR OF DOGS

This morning, as I was walking my neighbor's dog, it suddenly dawned on me how the Karen of my childhood would not even recognize me today. You see, I have (rather, *had*) a history of being afraid of dogs. Not just big dogs, like the Great Dane that I had on a leash today, but all dogs. My fear stemmed from a few different experiences I had growing up and even from something that happened before I was born!

The story goes that my family had a beagle named Peanuts. Apparently, Peanuts was a frisky puppy who got a little too rambunctious with one of my older sisters, and then the dog had to move to a new home. My parents vowed never to have a dog again. From then on, we were cat-people. Even though this was before my time, I was suspicious of dogs because I heard the story about Peanuts scratching poor Kathy and knocking her down! I assumed all dogs must be terrible if they do that to cute little toddlers, so parents have to give them away, and then whole families become cat-people! I didn't know anything about "puppy behaviors."

I also didn't spend much time around people with dogs, so I didn't know how to act around them. I didn't know which behaviors were regular dog behaviors and which ones meant "I'm going to eat you now!" Breathing noises were as frightening to me as growling noises, so I thought I would err on the side of safety and assume all dogs wanted to kill me. I adjusted my behaviors to match my expectations.

Then, when I was in seventh grade, a hunting dog escaped from his fenced yard just as I was walking to a friend's house, and the dog began to growl at me. Since I knew he wanted nothing more than to eat and destroy me, I screamed and ran like a lunatic! Guess what? The dog chased me and chased me until he bit onto my coat sleeve and practically tore it off. He stopped as soon as his owner came outside and called him back. I knew for sure at that point that dogs were evil.

A few years later, I was babysitting for a family who had an infant and a toddler. These two little girls lived in an enormous old house with big windows and two staircases. That evening, I put the girls to bed like always, closing their bedroom door behind me to keep out the drafts on this snowy December night. When I turned around, I saw a huge dog. I thought I must be crazy since the family didn't have any pets. After shaking my head and opening my eyes, the dog was still there and had now begun to growl at me. So I did the only thing that I knew to do. I ran.

I ran down the stairs as fast as possible, feeling so relieved that I had closed the bedroom door to the girls' room. No dingo was going to eat those babies!

But I was not so sure about myself. The dog literally pinned me to the sofa, growling and snapping his enormous jaws at me. I was sure I was dead. I quickly learned if I closed my eyes, the dog would merely breathe on me, saving his meal for later. So ironically, I played dead for the dog. For approximately six hours.

You will be glad to know there is a happy ending to this story. The parents were dog sitting for "Muffin" and just forgot to tell me. And I had quite a stack of money in my hands after they arrived home that night and heard my story!

As a teacher of young children, I am aware of how much children watch my reactions to them and to the world in general. I was fully aware that it would be just plain wrong to pass along my fear of dogs and, ultimately, make hun-

dreds of little children question whether dogs are evil creatures that only want to attack them. So I learned about
dogs. I asked families who had dogs to bring them to
school to teach us about dogs, including how to interact
with them and take care of them. I practiced standing by
dogs. I practiced petting dogs. I faced my fear.

So why am I sharing this story with you? To demonstrate
how fear can lead to poor decision-making, missed opportunities, and misunderstanding of the facts. Your children
might be fearful of dogs, spiders, or talking in front of a
group. Your children might be afraid to try a new sport,
invite a friend to the movies, or stand up for someone who
is being mistreated. How can you help your children find
their courage when they need it?

EMPOWERING THE CHILDREN

- Start with what your children know or think they know
  about the source of their fear. Correct any misconceptions they may have by providing facts. If you do not
  know the facts or the answer, honestly *tell* them you
  don't know the answer; then show them how to find
  the facts or answers or let them see you as you search
  for the answer. In my case, discovering why dogs sniff,
  drool, bark, growl, and chase things or people was the
  place to start.

- Teach coping skills. This activity could include instructing your children to take three deep breaths, put their
  hands together, or hold a charm kept in a pocket. Full

disclosure: I still have a tiny toy monkey that rides in the car with me or travels in my purse occasionally for extra support if I happen to need it! Who knew a two-inch monkey could help provide all the extra courage a grown-up might need?

- Practice the needed words, as they apply to your children's situation. For me, it was calming to think of all dogs as puppies and greet them with, "Hi, puppy!"

- Before the real dogs came to our classroom to visit, we practiced our dog skills with our large frisky dog puppet first! This is a good activity to do with children even if they are not afraid of dogs, but just lack experience with them.

- Learn the actions needed as they apply to your children's situation. For fear of dogs, instructions could be: stand like a tree, don't move, or ask the owner first if you can pet the dog. It's also useful to learn where to pet a dog and how to pet a dog.

- Be a good role model; kids pick up on your words and actions!

- Enlist support. Tell others what your children are working on and let them hold your child's hand, literally and figuratively.

ACTIVITY: FACING YOUR FEARS

- What has been holding you back from being the person you want to be? What are your fears? Why do they make you feel afraid?

- What is holding your children back from being the people they want to be? What are their fears? Why are they afraid?

- Let's help each other be courageous!

"It takes a great deal of bravery to stand up to your enemies, but a great deal more to stand up to your friends.

– Dumbledore,
Harry Potter and the Sorcerer's Stone

STANDING UP FOR WHAT'S RIGHT

Bullying Behaviors

In Chapter 3, I discussed in detail bullying behaviors. The point I want to make about bullying as it relates to courage is: The children who are bullied *and* the children who are showing bullying behaviors need to learn skills, with courage being one of them. Both sets of children are lacking skills in some way, both sets of children can learn these new skills, and both sets of children can move on. So what do we do to empower our children in these situations?

EMPOWERING THE CHILDREN

- For children who need help standing up for themselves, tell them that they are important. Tell them it is not okay for other people to treat them disrespectfully.

  ‣ Tell them what words they can say, such as "I don't like when you talk to me like that." "It hurts my body/feelings when you push me. I don't like it."

▸ Practice, practice, practice! Practice the words, practice in different settings (at home, in the car, at school, etc.), practice different scenarios. Let your children switch roles with you, too, so they can see a situation from more than one side.

▸ Do not treat your children like victims! This is a temporary skill-learning opportunity that will pass.

▸ Tell your child about times you were fearful and found your voice, your strength to stand up for yourself.

• For children who are doing the bullying behavior, keep in mind that they are hurting in some way, are trying to fill some need. Ask them what is going on, what they are afraid of. Listen. Listen some more.

▸ Ask your children how they feel before, during, and after they bully someone. See if you can replace their behaviors with more productive ones.

▸ Support your child by role-playing scenarios with their better behaviors.

▸ Do not treat your children like bullies! Their behavior is a temporary skill-learning opportunity that will pass.

▸ Tell your children about times when you did not act appropriately at first, but you learned how to manage your feelings, were courageous, and rectified the situation.

Courage is not the absence of fear, but rather the judgement that something else is more important than fear.
– Ambrose Redmoon

PEER PRESSURE AND WITNESSING INAPPROPRIATE ACTIVITIES

Just as fears can be learned by observation, so can courage. When children see the important people in their lives (parents, friends, relatives, teachers, etc.) model actions, children tend to repeat those actions, whether positive or negative.

EMPOWERING THE CHILDREN

- If you want your children to stand up for themselves, you need to stand up for yourself with your words and actions.

  - Do you talk respectfully about yourself? Your skills and abilities? Your appearance? Your personality?

  - Are you comfortable discussing your strengths and your weaknesses?

  - Do you vote in political elections to make your voice heard?

- If you want your children to stand up for those who can't stand up for themselves, you need to stand up for those same individuals with your words and actions.

  - How do you refer to other people with a different social or economic status from yourself? What terms do you use?

  - How do you treat those same people when you encounter them in your life? What words, if any, do you use? What does your body language say?

▸ How do you help those people meet their needs if they are unable to do it for themselves?

• If you want your children to stand up against the injustices they witness in the world, you need to stand up against the injustices you witness in the world with your words and actions.

▸ Are you informed about what is happening in your community? In the larger world around you?

▸ Do you discuss injustices with your children, asking them about their thoughts, and how they might find a solution to a problem?

▸ How are you involved in your community?

SUMMARY

Your children are constantly learning as they simply listen to and observe you. You can have a huge impact on them by your courageous example, by having one-on-one and group discussions, and by role-playing a variety of scenarios to help courage feel like a comfortable sweater.

Courage is what it takes to stand up and speak; courage is also what it takes to sit down and listen.
– Winston Churchill

CELEBRATING COURAGE
THROUGHOUT THE YEAR

★

January: International Child-Centered
                  Divorce Month

                  New Year's Resolution Week (1-4)

                  Someday We'll Laugh About This
                  Week (First week)

                  MLK Jr. Birthday Observed (21)

February: National Children's Dental
                  Health Month

                  International Expect Success Month

                  Youth Leadership Month

                  Freedom Day (1)

                  Rosa Parks' Birthday (4)

                  Inconvenience Yourself Day (27)

March: National Ethics Awareness Month

                  International Listening
                  Awareness Month

                  Optimism Month

                  Courageous Follower Day (4)

                  Middle Name Pride Day (8)

                  Awkward Moments Day (18)

April:	Card and Letter Writing Month
	Physical Wellness Month
	Weed Out Hate: Sow the Seeds of Peace Day (3)
May:	Heal the Children Month
	National Mental Health Month
	National Moving Month
	National Stuttering Awareness Month
	Young Achievers/Leaders of Tomorrow Month
	National Two Different Colored Shoes Day (3)
June:	Effective Communications Month
July:	National Make a Difference to Children Month
	Tell the Truth Day (7)
August:	Get Ready for Kindergarten Month
	National Immunization Awareness Month
September:	International People Skills Month
October:	Emotional Wellness Month
	National Bullying Prevention and Awareness Month

Positive Attitude Month

National Face Your Fears Day (8)

November: Cook Something Bold Day (8)

December: National Flashlight Day (28)

Chapter 10

Honesty

We tell lies when we are afraid...afraid of what we don't know, afraid of what others will think, afraid of what will be found out about us. But every time we tell a lie, the thing that we fear grows stronger.
– Tad Williams

Honesty. Is there more to honesty than not telling a lie to your parents, your teachers, or a friend? Can it be that simple?

To believe in something, and not to live it,
is dishonest.
– Mahatma Gandhi

MY FIRST LIE

I jumped out of bed and looked out the window to see what to wear to kindergarten. I was so excited! It had snowed overnight! I bundled up, ate breakfast, and headed out the door like always.

I began my roughly ten block trek to school, sliding on the sidewalks and making footprints along the way. After going about three blocks, I looked up and saw the biggest snow mountain I had ever seen in my entire life! I knew I *had* to go over it, not around it, on my way to school. What kid can resist a snow mountain?

I carefully crossed the street and happily began climbing up the face of my mountain. I was about halfway up when one of my legs began to slide deeper into the mountain. My adventure was getting even more exciting! I pushed harder with the other leg in order to pull my stuck leg out, only to find both legs wedged in even deeper.

Okay. No problem. Just pull the first leg harder. Nothing. I tried the second leg again. Still nothing. I looked around, searching for other people who might be outside, but the street was quiet. Eventually, I was able to dig my cold wet legs out of the snow. I crawled back down the mountain, tracing my original path back to the street.

I brushed all of the snow from my clothes and walked around the snow mountain. I continued on my way to school. Four blocks later, I came to the "busy intersection," the one that had a crossing guard to help us cross the street. But today, there was no crossing guard. I was too late because I had been stuck in the snow mountain for too long! I knew I wasn't supposed to cross this street without the crossing guard; plus I was scared to do it alone. My stomach began to hurt as I debated with myself about what I should do. I decided to go home and tell my mom I was sick.

I turned around and began walking home. I would be safe because I didn't cross the busy street. But I started to worry. What would I tell my mom? Would she be mad or disappointed in me because I went over the snow mountain instead of around it? Would she think I was just goofing around when I should have been walking to school? Should I have crossed the street anyway?

I opened the door to my house and walked in. My mom and little sister immediately came to see who was home. I burst out, "I don't feel good. My stomach hurts." Although this was true, it was because I didn't know what to do, not because I was sick like I told my mom. I didn't tell her about the snow mountain or the missing crossing guard. I let my mom help me out of my snowy clothes, and I climbed into bed. She covered me up, closed the curtains so I could sleep, and went downstairs. I stayed in bed all day, only coming downstairs for dinner when I decided I had miraculously recovered. (Reading this book might be the first time my mom finds out about this; if so, I'm sorry, Mom!)

I laid in bed all day still worrying. Was I bad for not telling my mom the truth? What would I do if the crossing guard weren't there tomorrow? I never really figured it out, but luckily for me, the crossing guard was always there when I needed him the rest of the school year.

EMPOWERING THE CHILDREN

- Children need to know what to do if they have questions, make mistakes, or don't understand what is going on. Prepare your children ahead of time by telling them about possible scenarios that might happen and come up with solutions they can try.

- Honesty is valued by most adults. Explain to kids why honesty is important to you. Tell them the consequences of not being honest. Sharing the story *The Boy Who Cried Wolf* is a great way to explain this concept to kids.

- Tell your kids about times when you did the difficult thing, were honest, and how that benefited your life or relationships.

Some people will not tolerate such emotional honesty in communication. They would rather defend their dishonesty on the grounds that it might hurt others. Therefore, having rationalized their phoniness into nobility, they settle for superficial relationships.
– Author Unknown

COWS CAN'T FLY

I read the book *Cows Can't Fly* by David Milgrim to my class before the kids went outside to play. In the book, a child draws a picture of cows flying. Adults in the story tell the child that cows can't fly and he should draw birds instead. A wind blows the drawing away, only to be found by some cows who look at the picture and teach themselves to fly. The child tries to point out the flying cows to a variety of adults, but they are too busy looking at the ground. The child begins to wonder what other things he can draw as the story ends.

The kids laughed as the events of this story unraveled. When it was time for them to line up to go outside, I asked each child what kind of flying creature he or she would be when we got outside. Their creative responses followed:

- Hugo was a cow car and asked to have his tires changed and tank filled with milk.

- Emile, who exclaimed that he was a unicorn, held a plastic cone to his forehead and asked us to tie a ribbon on his belt loop for a tail.

- Zoe was a unicorn pig.

- Cyrus was a seagull, holding a propeller in a cone that spun as he ran and flapped his arms.

- Chen was a race angel, which is even faster than a Blue Angel jet! He would run very fast and weave through other groups of children.

Cows Can't Fly can be a useful reminder to parents and teachers because it illustrates how children's creativity could easily be squashed unsuspectingly by simple adult comments or facts. The child in the book realizes that if you just take time to look up, lie back, and observe, many interesting things can be seen or created. This lesson is a good one for me to remember as a teacher of young children; grass does not have to be green, the sky does not always have to be up, and birds might not be the only animals you'll find flying today. In our efforts to teach what is right and correct, we might be squashing the creativity needed to solve many of the problems our communities face.

EMPOWERING THE CHILDREN

Just a moment to plant a seed and an idea can take root in different ways. Here are some seed-planting ideas:

- Differentiate between what is pretend and what is real life for your children. Not only does this process help them with issues related to honesty, but it will also help them understand the world better (media vs. reality).

- Introduce riddles to solve or silly situations to discover.

- Be good role models. Be aware of the little white lies you tell. How do you explain them to your children? Is it acceptable for them to do the same? Where is the line between an acceptable lie and an unacceptable lie? Perhaps a lesson in tactful communication vs. telling a white lie is in order instead.

- Tell your kids why the truth is important.

It's discouraging to think how many people are shocked by honesty and how few by deceit.
– Noel Coward

LEARNING ABOUT NATIVE AMERICANS

It was the month of Thanksgiving so we were learning about Native Americans and Pilgrims in our classroom. My co-teacher Jessica is Native American, so it was especially important for us to educate the children on some of the history of the Native Americans at the time of the Pilgrims and the first Thanksgiving as well as give them an idea of whom today's Native Americans are. This is an example of how stereotypes or inaccurate portrayals of history can make a difference in how a group of people were viewed in the past which in turn determines how they are treated in the present. Even at a young age, children can appreciate differences in cultures and the importance of honestly interacting with each other.

Our eighteen preschoolers sat around a real animal rug that was woven together to make a circle. On that rug, we placed a large drum in order to have a drum circle. Half of the children used wooden spoons covered with fabric to play the drum while the other children danced to the beat. I directed the children to play slowly, quickly, quietly, and then loudly, the dancing changing as the music changed. As I had discussed with the kids, when we counted "one... two...three," the drumming stopped and the dancers froze. It was time to switch roles.

Next, we investigated Native American artifacts that had been brought in to school for us to look at. We examined the rug more closely, noticing that it was laced together "Just like the canoes we made in the art area!" and was made from real deer fur. We discussed how the Native Americans used as much of the deer as possible for food, rugs, shoes, clothes, and tools after they shot it with a bow and arrow. We looked at the beautiful bead work on the moccasins and the feathers on the fan used for dancing ceremonies. The colorful beaded cloth with the fringe felt silky and smooth to the touch and moved in a pretty way when we danced with it.

At story time, we talked about how the Native Americans did not have books like we have. They verbally told stories, often while looking at the stars. These stories frequently were about the stars and what the Native Americans saw in the sky. So we all lay on our backs with our heads on the rug, pretending to look in the sky. I read our book about the night sky to the kids, walking around the circle of children and holding the pictures over their heads, just like they were looking into the sky at a nighttime constellation.

We briefly discussed how more and more Europeans came to America by ship and wanted to live here. The new Americans liked the area where the Native Americans were already living, so they wanted the Native Americans to move away to give them more room to live. People tried to trick the Native Americans by giving them cheap trinkets instead of a fair amount of money for the land, too. Big fights broke out and lots of Native Americans died and were pushed away from their homes. We brought up the discussion point "What would you do today if you wanted to live on the nice land that someone else already lived on, or someone else had something that you wanted?"

EMPOWERING THE CHILDREN

- Ask your children what they think about situations such as these:

  ▸ What would you do today if you wanted to live on the land that someone else already lived on, or someone else had something that you wanted? Is that fair? Why or why not?

  ▸ What would you do today if someone wanted to live on the land that you already lived on, or you had something that he or she wanted? Is that fair? Why or why not?

▸ How could you come up with a plan that makes both sides happy instead of having a big fight?

▸ Do you think it is okay to trick someone to get what you want instead of asking for it honestly? Is that fair? Why or why not?

Those who think it is permissible to tell white lies soon grow color-blind.
– Austin O'Malley

SUMMARY

Honesty is much more than telling the truth to your parents or teachers. It involves being honest with yourself and being the type of person others trust. It involves trusting your judgment, your own eyes, and acting with integrity. It involves making amends for past transgressions and preventing future ones.

CELEBRATING HONESTY
THROUGHOUT THE YEAR

★

January: National Be On Purpose Month

               National Compliment Day (24)

February: Library Lovers' Month

               National Black History Month

               National Mend a Broken Heart Month

               Worldwide Renaissance of the
               Heart Month

March: Humor Society Awareness Month

               International Ideas Month

               National Ethics Awareness Month

               Middle Name Pride Day (8)

               Panic Day (9)

               True Confessions Day (15)

April: Emotional Overeating Awareness Month

               National Card and Letter
               Writing Month

               National Take a Wild Guess Day (15)

               National Honesty Day (30)

May: Family Wellness Month

June:	Flip a Coin Day (1)
July:	National Make a Difference to Children Month
	Tell the Truth Day (7)
August:	Get Ready for Kindergarten Month
September:	College Savings Month
	National Coupon Month
October:	Emotional Wellness Month
	National Bullying Prevention and Awareness Month
November:	National American Indian Heritage Month
December:	Card Playing Day (28)

Chapter 11

Caring

★

Too often we underestimate the power of a touch, a smile, a kind word, a listening ear, an honest compliment, or the smallest act of caring, all of which have the potential to turn a life around.
– Leo F. Buscaglia

Sometimes caring means caring about those we know and love, and sometimes it means caring about people in a broader sense. There are people in our neighborhoods and schools who are friends we haven't met yet, people in our communities whom we see but don't know, and people who live on the other side of the world whom we probably won't ever meet, but we know they are humans like us. How do we get kids to care about people outside of their everyday lives?

Walk with the dreamers, the believers, the courageous, the cheerful, the planners, the doers, the successful people with their heads in the clouds and their feet on the ground. Let their spirit ignite

a fire within you to leave this world better than
when you found it.
– Unknown

PEACE IS POSSIBLE

The first way to teach children to care about others is by believing that peace in the world is possible. Not in a hippy,
flowers in the hair, new-age sort-of-way, but in real life.
We are often told that wars are inevitable, that there are
no possible ways to reach an agreement between "us" and
"them." We are too different from each other and will never
see eye-to-eye. "They" are the "evil-doers" while we are on
the "moral path." If we think about it, "they" see "us" in the
exact same way, but from their perspective, we are the evil-
doers and they are the ones who are on the morally correct
path. Thinking this way does make it seem like war, fighting, and permanent disagreement is the real truth.

But in fact, wars begin because someone in power makes
the decision to go to war. It is a choice from a set of op-
tions. There have been other times in history when problems seemed insurmountable and the path unalterable,
yet changes were made. These changes were made from
the ground up; they came from the people. Three great
examples of such changes include abolishing the enslave-
ment of our African-American population, the Civil Rights
Movement, and giving women the right to vote. In each
case, both sides seemed resolved not to break. But with a
change in ideas eventually came a change of heart. The next
step led to the enacting of laws to make sure that slavery

was illegal, civil rights were a matter of law, and women could vote, with consequences in place for breaking these laws.

Does a law mean everyone believes slavery is wrong or that women should be allowed to vote? Not necessarily. But what matters is that there is a law in place to prevent slavery in the future and a law in place to protect women's rights to vote. Now most people can't imagine a world where either scenario is common practice.

I can remember wondering how people were able to change the minds of the masses and inspire them to join the effort to make these changes possible. I can also remember almost falling out of my chair when I discovered that the efforts of less than 1 percent of the U.S. population made each of these groundbreaking achievements a reality! Less than 1 percent of the population getting involved in a case that was important to them applied enough political pressure to change major U.S. policy. Ordinary citizens can and do revolutionize seemingly unchangeable systems by taking a stand, by drawing a line in the sand, and saying, "We refuse to cross this line." Paul K. Chappell[1] reiterates that landmark changes occur "Not because everyone participated in it, but because a small percentage of the population was willing to wage peace and make a difference."

---

1 Paul Chappell, a well-known author and the Nuclear Age Peace Foundation's Peace Leadership Program Director, made this comment when he spoke at the Peace Leadership Training Summer Workshop I attended in July 2012 in Santa Barbara, California.

Additionally, if we want to have peace in our world, we must study war and killing in the same way a doctor studies disease to be better able to cure a sick person. At first, this comparison may sound a little bit strange. But what if a doctor only studied optimal health, hoping that would lead to producing healthy patients? We would think that was absurd and search for a better trained doctor. Likewise, if we desire peace, we need to study war and killing in order to understand the causes, symptoms, risk factors, costs, and treatments. Only then do we have a chance at finding a cure or preventative measures that will provide us with peace.

Often, we shy away from things that are unpleasant, scary, or disturbing, but if we truly want to solve this problem, we need to understand its underlying causes and not just treat an unrelated symptom, which at best is ineffective, and at worst, unwittingly causes even more serious problems. As peace advocates, we must learn about war to be effective in our efforts. As parents and educators, we owe such efforts to our children and the future we leave to them.

Whenever elections approach, we can elect leaders who will not glorify war or put people in harm's way to advance politics or for ideological reasons. War as a means of national defense should refer to self-defense when invaded inside our borders by other nations. Political leaders must acknowledge that the costs of war are enormous (in terms of human and financial sacrifice) and we cannot control the outcome, no matter how skilled our military forces and leaders are. Thus any use of force would need intense scrutiny and acceptance by the people.

EMPOWERING THE CHILDREN

To care about other people, you must understand them. To understand them, you must see how you are similar to each other. Here are some ways to bring about this understanding with your children:

- Discuss how we are all part of our families. Children have parents, parents have parents. Parents love their children, want to take care of them, and want their children to be healthy and successful in life.

- Role play different points of view in any given situation.

- Remember that prejudices are born from observing others' words and actions, and children pick up on these things from age three and up.

Being considerate of others will take your children further in life than any college degree.
– Marian Wright Edelman

ONE DUCK STUCK

After our classroom learned about other people who did not have as much as we have, the kids were very interested in finding more ways to help other people. Jessica and I wanted to make sure that the children did not just feel sorry for the people and feel like they were not capable people, but rather, that they understood these people were victims of circumstance. We did some investigation and decided to support the local charity World Vision.

World Vision, and a similar charity, Heifer International, will provide living animals to families as tools to help them meet their economic needs. For example, chickens can lay eggs, which can be used for food, or sold or bartered for other goods or services. Sheep can provide wool for clothing, milk that can also be made into cheese and yogurt, and baby sheep that can bring additional income when sold. Because our group of kids loved learning about animals and pretending to be animals so much, this charity seemed a natural fit.

The next task? How to raise money to purchase animals for families in need. We remembered the book *One Duck Stuck* by Phyllis Root, in which teamwork by a group of animals was required to free the duck who was stuck in the muck. This story seemed to be perfect for us to perform as a play!

The children made tickets with drawings and stickers on them to give to audience members as they arrived. They made animal costumes and scenery. On performance days, they showed the catalog to interested adults and kids, telling them which animals they hoped to give to families in other parts of the world as they accepted donations. They answered questions from the audience after the shows. Four performances and hundreds of dollars later, we purchased the following: chickens, ducks, rabbits, a sheep, a goat, a share (money toward) a plow and ox, and a share of a cow!

EMPOWERING THE CHILDREN

When your children care about others or the world they live in, it is important to find ways to allow them to share their care and passion. Putting on a play is only one idea. Here are some others:

- Collect litter as you go on a walk.

- Carry granola bars, apples, or bottles of water in the car or your backpack. Share with homeless people or others you normally walk or drive past.

- Collect food for the food bank.

- Donate toys and clothes for homeless shelters. Some even specialize in families with children, so they would really appreciate these items.

- Visit soup kitchens and see whether your children can help serve food, wash tables, pass out napkins, read stories, or sing a song for entertainment. You would need to stay with your children during these activities.

- Make cookies and give them to an elderly person down the block.

- Invite new neighbors to dinner.

- Read stories to people of all ages in the hospital.

- Take your neighbor's dog for a walk.

- Share a bit of nature with someone you love. A flower, leaf, or rock can bring joy to someone who doesn't get outside as much as he or she would like.

- Give hugs to friends and neighbors.

- Hand out drawings or smiley faces to strangers.

Live so that when your children think of fairness,
caring, and integrity, they think of you.
– H. Jackson Brown, Jr.

NOT JUST AN EARTHQUAKE

On March 11, 2011, a devastating earthquake and tsunami hit Japan. Halfway across the world in Seattle, this event was big news. Many people had ties to Japan, and the rest of us had tremendous empathy for the survivors.

As was typical, children saw images on TV and in the newspapers, heard parents and teachers talking about it, and grew concerned themselves. In my classroom, some kids brought in photos and stories from the paper to share with us. We looked at the photos, told the stories, and answered questions as best we could.

One of the most common questions was, "What can we do to help?" It would have been easy to brush off these preschoolers, telling them that they were too little, lived too far away, or couldn't do something big enough to make a difference. Instead, Jessica and I decided to see what they wanted to do to help, so we could help to support their efforts.

Because we had raised money in the past for the purchase of animals for families to use for income and food sources, the kids wanted to raise money again. Last time, we did a play based on a book, so we thought we'd write our own original play this time. We used the newspaper articles as the basis of our storytelling, creating a play that would help to educate people about what happened as well as raise money.

We made a display with the newspaper clippings and our drawings about this natural disaster for the audience to look at. We performed the play, including buckling roads, collapsing buildings, and the crushing tsunami wave. We included true stories about a man floating on his roof, the store owner who gave food away, and people patiently lining up for bottled water. We answered questions from the audience, including why the victims needed bottled water, how a tsunami is created, and how rescue dogs can help in an emergency.

We raised about $500 with our four performances of *Not Just an Earthquake*. We gave the money to a charity that would provide food, water, and activities for children while in transition.

If you think you are too small to be effective, you have never been in bed with a mosquito.
– Betty Reese

NOT JUST AN EARTHQUAKE: An Original Play

It was an ordinary day, a regular day in Japan.

- People were driving cars home from work.
- Children were walking home from school.
- Some people were at home with their families.

Then the ground began to rumble a little. Then it rumbled a lot!

- The people fell to the ground.
- Some of the cars crashed.
- The buildings shook, then fell apart.
- The roads shook and buckled and broke in half.
- Many people were trapped in the rubble.

Then something else happened. It was not just an earthquake.

- The ground stopped shaking. A huge tsunami wave rose high in the water and crashed on the ground, washing many things away.
  - ▸ Buildings, cars, and people.
  - ▸ A man even floated away on the roof of his house!

Now it was time for some real-life heroes!

- Rescue workers used their eyes to look for people and listened with their ears for people calling for help.
- Rescue dogs used their super sniffers to help find people too.

When the rescue workers found people who needed help, they did many things.

- They checked to see whether they were okay and put bandages on their injuries.
- Sometimes they had to give sad news to the people.
  - ▸ "I'm sorry, but your cat died in the earthquake."
- Then it was time to make sure the people had food to eat and water to drink.
  - ▸ They asked the people to make a line and get their water.
  - ▸ Some store owners told the people to come in and take some food, and they didn't have to pay for it.
- Now the rescue workers wondered, "Where will the people live who do not have homes anymore?"
  - ▸ They set up shelters for the people to stay in.
  - ▸ The people were grateful for the help.

Even though the shaking has stopped and the tsunami wave is gone, the people of Japan still need our help.

- We would like to collect money for a local charity.
- The charity will give food and clothes to the people.
- And make sure kids have a safe place to play.

EMPOWERING THE CHILDREN

- Explain to the children what happened in terms they can understand.

- Show the kids on a map where they are and where the disaster occurred to help them understand they are safe.

- Tell the kids how you are prepared for disasters (fires, earthquakes, tornados, etc.) and practice the drills regularly.

- Help the kids to demonstrate their compassion and caring. If they want to make a donation or perform another act of caring, show them how to accomplish it.

- Be a role model for helping and caring about those in need.

Kindness is the language which the deaf can hear and the blind can see.
– Mark Twain

SUMMARY

Sometimes it takes a tragic event to open our eyes to the plight of another person and that awakens empathy and caring. Sometimes, we learn to be caring by watching how the important people in our lives treat others and ourselves, especially when we are not at our best. Our most challenging moments, when someone is least lovable in our eyes, and how we choose to act are the times when we can be the most effective teachers for our children.

CELEBRATING CARING
THROUGHOUT THE YEAR

★

January: Be Kind to Food Servers Month

                National Mentoring Month

                Poverty in America Awareness Month

                National Volunteer Blood Donor
                Month

                National Hugging Day (21)

February: Bake for Family Fun Month

                National Mend a Broken Heart Month

                Plant the Seeds of Greatness Month

                Random Acts of Kindness Week
                (Second week)

                World Day for Social Justice (20)

March: International Listening Awareness
                Month

                National Humor Month

                Sing With Your Child Month

                Johnny Appleseed Day (11)

                Good Samaritan Involvement Day (13)

                Forgive Mom and Dad Day (18)

                Absolutely Incredible Kid Day (21)

National Puppy Day (23)

April: Month of the Young Child

National Card and Letter Writing Month

National Donate Life Month

National Day of Hope (3)

National Love Our Children Day (6)

National Siblings Day (10)

World Healing Day (27)

May: Family Wellness Month

Gifts from the Garden Month

National Inventors' Month

PTA Teacher Appreciation Week (First week)

National Teacher Day (7)

Donate a Day's Wages to Charity Day (8)

Letter Carriers "Stamp Out Hunger" Food Drive (11)

June: Adopt-A-Shelter-Cat Month

National Hunger Awareness Month

Hunger Day (6)

July: Cell Phone Courtesy Month

National Make a Difference to Children Month

Tell the Truth Day (7)

August: National Win With Civility Month

What Will Be Your Legacy Month

September: International People Skills Month

National Courtesy Month

October: Adopt-A-Shelter-Dog Month

Celebrating the Bilingual Child Month

Disability Employment Awareness Month

Diversity Awareness Month

National Bullying Prevention and Awareness Month

Positive Attitude Month

World Smile Day (4)

World Teachers' Day (5)

World Humanitarian Action Day (8)

World Blind Day/World Sight Day (15)

White Cane Safety Day (15)

International Stuttering Awareness Day (22)

National Forgiveness Day (26)

National Make a Difference Day (27)

November: National Adoption Awareness Month

National American Indian & Alaska Native Heritage Month

Latin American Month

National Hunger & Homelessness Awareness Month

National Inspirational Role Models Month

World Freedom Day (9)

World Kindness Day (13)

National Hunger & Homelessness Awareness Week (week before Thanksgiving)

December: Universal Human Rights Month

Chapter 12

Trust

★

Trust is like paper. Once it's crumpled it can never
be perfect again.
– Unknown

Trust is a simple five-letter word. It is very fragile and extremely strong at the same time. Trust can be a very difficult
concept to teach children, yet so powerful when children
know they are trusted. Equally powerful and important is
the need for children to have important people in their lives
whom they can trust in return; they need to trust these people to be there for them, take care of them, and simply love
them for whom they are at this very moment.

How do you explain trust to children and teach them to
trust? With extremely little ones, it means responding to
them when they cry. Talking to them, touching them, acknowledging them, holding them if possible. Sometimes it
isn't possible to drop everything each and every time young
children cry, but the first step is acknowledging them in
some way, shape, or form and making them aware that you

hear them and you are on your way. Letting tiny ones cry it out leads to children who stop crying for help, who don't ask for help, even when they truly need it later in life.

I can't recall where I first came across the following story, but it illustrates another point. We build trust in others by loving them, guiding them, and holding on to them, both literally and figuratively. We can't expect them automatically to trust us back.

A little girl and her father were crossing a bridge. The father was kind of scared so he asked his little daughter: "Sweetheart, please hold my hand so you don't fall into the river."

The little girl said: "No, Dad. You hold my hand."

"What's the difference?" asked the puzzled father.

"There's a big difference," replied the little girl. "If I hold your hand and something happens to me, chances are that I may let your hand go. But if you hold my hand, I know for sure that no matter what happens, you will never let my hand go."

In any relationship, the essence of trust is not in its bind, but in its bond. So hold the hand of the person you love rather than expecting her to hold yours....

It is an equal failing to trust everybody,
and to trust nobody.
– English Proverb

SHOULD WE ALLOW OUR KIDS TO GO FREE-RANGE?

I was recently in Kauai, Hawaii on a relaxing vacation with my husband. We spent as much time as possible snorkeling at the beaches, exploring the small towns, and hiking and boating around the "Garden Isle," most familiar to mainlanders from the movies *Pirates of the Caribbean*, *Raiders of the Lost Ark*, and *Jurassic Park*.

In addition to the amazing scenery, delicious Kahlua pork, and "the best coconut shrimp on the planet" (Thank you, Shrimp Station!), I noticed something that was occurring regularly on this island of 60,000 people with 1.2 million annual visitors, something peculiar compared to what I normally see, and it evoked strong emotions in me.

On one of my first days of vacation, I saw a young teenager on the beach. My first thought was "Where is his family?" I felt like I was keeping an extra eye on this thirteen- or fourteen-year-old young man. Why? As I said, he was probably thirteen or fourteen years old. I was babysitting a family's three little ones when I was ten, so why was I concerned about a boy who was three or four years older than that? The teenager spent his time relaxing in the sun, snacking on fruit and appeared to be exploring the shells and vegetation on the beach. He didn't even get in the water. Was I afraid someone would kidnap him? This beach was occupied only by my husband and me and just one other couple snorkeling. We had to hike about fifteen minutes to arrive at this secluded beach. If a predator really wanted to kidnap a child, the probability of finding one down here alone was remote, and this boy willingly would have to hike himself back up from the beach; not an easy grab and go situation!

Another day, as we were driving to an early morning boat trip locale, we passed four individual elementary aged girls riding their bikes to school. Each one had a small grin on her face as she rode. Was it the freedom? The breeze blowing in their young faces? The joy of physical activity early in the morning hours? We also passed kids walking to school individually or in pairs. Where were the adults?

Later, we ate lunch at a neighborhood cafe attended by local patrons. Sitting at the table next to me was a father and his two-and-a-half-year-old son. The boy, who told me his name was Matthew, was finished with his meal and his father was just beginning to enjoy his refilled drink. Matthew jumped up from the table and walked to the door, which was between our tables. Matthew walked out the open door and onto the attached porch, immediately turned around, and returned to his father, exclaiming, "I'm back!" and giving a high-five. This game was repeated numerous times, each time with Matthew's father allowing him the opportunity to walk out the door to the porch, and then return on his own after ten to thirty seconds. The waitress at the cafe also gave Matthew high-fives and allowed him to explore without any reminder to stay with his dad.

A few days passed and we were at Hanalei Bay. As we walked to the pier to snap a few photos, we passed a young boy, who was probably two years old, next to the ocean surf with a surfboard beside him. The boy spent time playing with the surfboard, repeatedly putting the Velcro cuff on his ankle and trying to drag the surfboard into the water to no avail. This future surfer would run along the shore and pull on the surfboard again and again, until he needed to lay on the sand for a break. Then repeat. The boy played his game for the thirty minutes we were there without direct interaction or intervention from the four adults chatting together nearby. It was unclear to me who was this child's parent, but the boy seemed confident and content while the adults appeared relaxed and aware.

What was happening on this beautiful island? I took advantage of the time I had the captain and his assistant's attention during our boat ride to ask them about their views on parenting on an island that was both "small town" and had many tourists, thus an exceptional number of "strangers." The assistant was a twenty-year-old native of Kauai who now attends college in San Diego. He said that it was "like growing up in a village where everyone knows each other and looks out for each other, so parents don't have to be watching you all the time." The captain stated, "I need my kids to be able to make decisions and learn how to do things for themselves. How can they do that if I do it for them all the time?" He was also clearly grateful to the tourists who provide his family and the other locals with their livelihood; tourists did not imply stranger danger.

Coincidentally, I just happened to be reading *Free-Range Kids: Giving Our Children the Freedom We Had Without Going Nuts with Worry*. These examples all illustrate the concepts outlined in this popular book, written by Lenore Skenazy after she came to fame and was labeled "America's Worst Mom" by allowing her nine-year-old son to ride the subway alone in New York City. He had been begging for this opportunity for months, and Skenazy and her husband (who was not vilified, by the way) discussed and agreed that their son was ready for this responsibility. She prepared her son for this hour-long trip. He had a map, $20 in cash, and coins for a payphone. (She knew her cell phone would be too distracting for him!) As prearranged, Skenazy left her son at Bloomingdale's and met him at home on that Sunday afternoon.

When Skenazy shared this adventure with her friends and other moms, they told her she was crazy and irresponsible. She ended up on the talk show circuit, finding her trust in her child to be a hot-button issue. She decided to write her book to address the real dangers to children today vs. hype, the fear-mongering by the media, outright bad information fed to parents and teachers, and modern-day myths about child safety. She also addresses how this radical change in our view of society happened. Skenazy insists, "Mostly, the world is safe. Mostly, people are good," and she wants her children to know it.

First of all, Skenazy says the statistics of child abduction do not match the time, effort, and fear parents put into worrying about this issue. According to Warwick Cairns, British author of *How to Live Dangerously*, "If you actually wanted your child to be kidnapped and held overnight by a stranger, how long would you have to keep her outside, unattended, for this to be statistically likely to happen? About seven hundred and fifty thousand years." This number can be converted to a .00007 percent chance of any one American child being kidnapped and killed by a stranger.

So does Skenazy advocate letting our kids run loose without supervision? No. Each child must be looked at as an individual, and parents and teachers must assess his or her strengths and weaknesses. We owe it to our kids to allow them to gain self-confidence as they stretch themselves, trying to create and master new skills on the road to independence. We can do it one "mini-lesson" at a time to help them grow their wings and to give *ourselves* the confidence to let go a little and trust our children, trust in the good of the world.

I know if you asked the children who were in my classroom what our #1 Rule was, they would all say, "Safety first!" For us, safety meant looking before crossing the street, holding the butter knife by the handle, sitting while chewing and swallowing your food, and using walking feet in the classroom. It is not a call to be overly worried that danger is lurking around every corner, but to be aware of what you are doing and making good choices to the best of your abilities.

Put another way, the term free-range, when applied to animal husbandry, means a method where the animals are allowed to roam freely instead of being contained in any manner (outside the U.S.) or that the animal has been allowed access to the outside (in the U.S.). According to Skenazy, many young adults complain that as children they were overprotected and felt like "captives" who could not go outside (only 30 percent of today's children play outside compared to 70 percent of their parents' generation). As young adults, they report fear of trying new things, fear of failure, and fear that they are not capable of solving their own problems.

EMPOWERING THE CHILDREN

Empowering children to feel trusted by us follows very closely upon helping them learn to be safe in their world. More specifically, we need to provide them with opportunities to practice their skills of being safe each day by showing that we trust them. For suggestions on how to do this, please refer to the activities listed after "Safety First!" in Chapter 1.

> The inability to open up to hope is what blocks trust, and blocked trust is the reason for blighted dreams.
> – Elizabeth Gilbert

With trust, not only do we need to trust the children, but we need them to learn to trust themselves to do the right thing. How do you teach children about self-trust? How do you trust that you've done your job so you can be confident that your children can make strong decisions that will help them to be successful individuals?

In Chapter 7, I discussed how saying *no* to your children can help them learn to say no to themselves when temptation is present and adults are not there to lend support. I was interested in trying my own Marshmallow Experiment in my classroom to see how prepared the three to five year olds in my care were and how I could be more confident they were on their way toward success.

MY MARSHMALLOW EXPERIMENT

"The Marshmallow Experiment" is a famous scientific experiment originally done with four year olds in 1972. My version was less scientific; the original had one child isolated in a room with nothing to do except hang out with the marshmallow. The researcher watched on closed circuit TV for up to fifteen minutes.

Due to time and room constraints, I needed to modify it.

I brought the Trailblazer kids (eighteen preschoolers, ages three to five) to the empty snack table, four at a time. I asked them to sit down for a "Marshmallow Experiment." I gave each child a tiny cup containing three mini-marshmallows. I said, "You can have all of these marshmallows to eat. But if you wait for five minutes, I will give you another cup of mini-marshmallows with six marshmallows in it. You can then eat all nine marshmallows. If you decide not to wait, you can eat your three marshmallows and leave the table."

Here is how the children responded:

- Children who kept their hands in their laps, at their sides, or under their arms: fifteen

- Children who waited quietly: ten, two of whom watched the clock.

- Children who smelled the marshmallows: two, one who did so after being told to smell them by another child. (Interestingly, the follower said smelling it made it more difficult for her to wait.)

- Children who played with the marshmallows: one

- Children who talked while waiting: six. They said things like:

  - "I'll just be patient even though it'll be hard."

  - "Is it time yet?"

  - "Shh! Quiet!"

  - "This is so hard!"

  - "I'm waiting. I'm waiting."

  - "I'm waiting. I'm not waiting."

- Children who waited: seventeen

  - Children who reported it was easy to wait: fifteen

- Children who didn't wait: one

  - This child repeated constantly "I'm waiting. I'm not waiting" and gave in after ninety seconds.

  - This child said it wasn't fair that she couldn't have the extra marshmallows, even though she knew how the game worked.

  - I told her she could try again in three days, and I knew she'd be able to wait the whole time. And she did!

  - She sat quietly the second time and occasionally said, "I'm waiting." She dropped her negative self-talk!

- Children who said it was hard to wait: four

What techniques did these young kids report using to make waiting easier for themselves?

- Talking to themselves or out loud.

- Watching the clock.

- Sniffing the marshmallows.

- Touching the marshmallows.

- "Waiting is easy because you just use your patience."

- Researchers also have learned that teaching children to visualize the marshmallows as fluffy clouds and not delicious treats also helps.

I personally was surprised that I didn't have to elaborate what I meant by "techniques" to the kids. These preschoolers were aware that they already have strategies that they employ, or have in their toolbox, when needed.

The importance of peer relations cannot be underestimated. Some children appeared to gain strength from each other's presence. Others seemed to find it distracting. This difference may be important to keep in mind as a parent for a few reasons:

- When children begin school and have homework to complete, some may need quiet spots with few distractions (visual and auditory) in order to do their best work.

- Children may be easily led by peer pressure, and being able to say no or yes in appropriate situations when parents are not present is crucial.

It's amazing how much people can get done if they don't worry about who gets the credit.
– Sandra Swinney

TEAMWORK

When children know the important adults in their lives trust them to try new tasks and reach goals, or to accomplish things for themselves, they in turn learn to trust themselves. When children learn to trust their own inner voice, they are able to trust themselves when they find themselves in tempting situations and are better able to say *no* to peer pressure. But we ideally want children to see the value in trusting other people as well, and that it is okay to need other people for support, camaraderie, and help when they need it. Neither do we want them to look down upon others who may need help. We do not live in a fair world in which all children are born at the same starting line. It is not fair to discriminate against others because they were born behind or in front of our starting point, or simply because they are different from us.

We often want to withhold our trust of someone until that person earns it from us. But that is a pessimistic point of view to take. Why not trust other people unless a specific person proves untrustworthy instead? Why label entire groups based upon the actions of one person at one specific time?

Evidence shows that a small number of strangers have done terrible things to children. Evidence also shows that much larger numbers of children are injured in car accidents or by family members. Yet our society has a huge fear of strangers harming children.

If we were to compare the benefits of teaching your children how to interact with strangers and others by trusting them to help others, the gains would be huge for both sides. Children would learn responsibility for their surroundings and belongings, would improve their communication skills, and would know how to act in a real emergency rather than just be afraid. Others would be proud to help another in need, become more aware of their own surroundings, improve their communication skills, and practice their emergency skills. Win-win!

EMPOWERING THE CHILDREN

How do we teach interdependence through trust? Teamwork!

- Define your role or job to your children and their roles or jobs in any given situation. Be clear in your definitions! For example, if you are going to the grocery store, talk ahead of time about how you will push the cart and read the grocery list; your children will take items from the shelves and put them in the cart. Teamwork!

    ▸ Also discuss how all people eat food so there will probably be a lot of people at the store. In order to make sure you don't mix up kids with another family (little joke!), you will trust your children to stay where they can see you and the shopping cart. By saying "where they (your children) can see you," you give them a little responsibility to stay aware of their location, although as the parent *you* are really responsible for your children.

    ▸ Discuss and role play what to do if you got separated from each other. Suggestions?

        ▸▸ Point out what the employees look like. Do they have uniforms or nametags? Is there a person at a cash register?

▸▸ Point out what other parents look like. This is easy because they have kids with them and they know how to help kids!

▸▸ Practice how to get an adult's attention in a busy place that may be noisy or if the adult is not expecting interaction from a child he or she hasn't met yet.

  • Say "Excuse me."

  • Tap the adult on the arm.

  • Use a strong, loud voice.

  • Say, "Can you help me find my parent?"

  • Switch roles with your children so they can see what it feels like to be a child who has lost a parent, a store employee or parent they haven't met yet, or a worried parent who has lost a child. You can also practice this exercise at school for field trips.

• If your children tend to get distracted in public spaces and it stresses you out, lighten up the situation with a little humor as you remind them to pull the cotton (or socks, whatever works for your children) out of their ears so they can hear your words. Do the same with your ears, and try not to laugh as you "pull" out yards and yards of fluff together!

• Are you demonstrating that you trust others to help you when you need it? This is particularly difficult for those of us with perfectionist tendencies, but it is great for teaching how to trust in others' capabilities, talents, and motives.

- We all have prejudices in how we look at the world and others in it. What matters is our actions. Examine your own prejudices. What messages are you teaching your children about the world and specific groups of people or animals in it? Are you unwittingly teaching them to distrust nature, men, certain races or political parties, people with facial hair or tattoos, snakes, smart people, poor people, rich people, etc? Revise your actions if needed.

- Allow your children to spend time with others (or things) they do not trust due to lack of experience to find similarities or beauty in their existence. Set up time in nature for those fearful of nature. Invite teamwork opportunities to those in conflict.

  ‣ Plant trees or flowers.

  ‣ Carry large items together or play a game that requires two people.

  ‣ Have a play date together.

Interdependence is and ought to be as much the ideal of man as self-sufficiency.
– Gandhi

SUMMARY

In order to help children reach their full potential, parents and teachers must be sensitive to the impact and importance of the development of trust in their lives. From the very beginning, infants need to know that someone is there, hearing their calls for food, nurturing them, and helping them learn to regulate their systems. If infants are ignored, many give up trying to be part of the greater community before they can even speak. Their lack of trust keeps them from feeling comfortable in the world as well as in their own skin.

By learning to trust in the world, children begin to trust in themselves. They learn that they can say no to things that can harm their bodies and minds. They eventually are able to combine their trust with confidence and courage, standing up for things larger than themselves, and those without a voice.

Children who trust are able to see how trust is an integral part of life. It allows for full participation in life, with confidence, in a variety of situations with any number of people. Trust leads to better cooperation and problem-solving with others, thus leading to a richer experience in life.

CELEBRATING TRUST
THROUGHOUT THE YEAR

★

January: Get Organized Month

International Child-Centered
Divorce Awareness Month

National Mentoring Month

Inauguration Day (20)

February: Bake for Family Fun Month

International Boost Self-Esteem Month

International Expect Success Month

National Parent Leadership Month

National Time Management Month

Relationship Wellness Month

Youth Leadership Month

Great Backyard Bird Count (15-18)

My Way Day (17)

March: International Ideas Month

International Listening
Awareness Month

Optimism Month

Middle Name Pride Day (8)

Panic Day (9)

April: National Child Abuse
                   Prevention Month

                   National Day of Hope (3)

                   National Love Our Children Day (6)

May: Family Wellness Month

                   International Civility Awareness Month

                   Young Achievers/Leaders of
                   Tomorrow Month

                   Loyalty Day (1)

                   National Learn to Swim Day (18)

June: Effective Communications Month

July: National Make a Difference to
                   Children Month

                   Tell the Truth Day (7)

August: Getting Ready for Kindergarten Month

                   Happiness Happens Month

September: Starting School/Changing Schools

                   International People Skills Month

                   International Self-Awareness Month

                   International Strategic Thinking Month

                   Library Card Sign-Up Month

October: International Skeptics Day (13)

November: National Adoption Month

December: Make Up Your Mind Day (31)

Final Notes

★

Now that we have reached the end of this book, you have a decision to make. Are you ready to empower your children? Remember, you don't have to do all of these suggestions every day, but you do have to be committed to being a good role model and selecting a couple of items to focus on at a time. As stated in the Introduction, there are many ideas to choose from and a variety of ways to use this book as a resource:

- Pick one chapter or topic to focus on. Is there an area that your children are struggling with? Do you want to help your children develop a particular quality more deeply? Begin there.

- Do you want to work on a variety of skill areas over the course of the year? Look at the end of each chapter to see how you and your family can celebrate throughout the year. Choose holidays that appeal to you and your children. Do you like to play games? Take the Million Minute Family Challenge (September 1-December 31) and spend one million minutes playing games together. Do you like to do silly things together? Celebrate Bubble Wrap Appreciation Day (January 28) or Take Your Houseplants for a Walk Day (July 27). If there is a holiday you like and miss the day, celebrate it on a different day! Make up your own unique family specific holidays! Google the holidays if you want more information on specific ones.

- Research shows that it takes twenty-one days to make something a habit. Give yourself time to practice new skills, just like you give your children time to practice and learn. The goal is to add to our toolbox, so we have more tools available to choose from for different situations. No one tool works for every circumstance, just like your hammer will never work to screw something in no matter how skilled you are at hammering!

Let's summarize our values that lead to successful children:

The safety of our children is the foundation that we build upon. Keep in mind that we want to empower children to learn how to be responsible in the world, how to question, and how to make good decisions. We want them to be confident, not overly concerned about unrealistic concerns. We need to educate our children; then allow them to participate.

Health is another building block in our foundation for successful children. Physical health includes exercise, nutrition, sleep, and preventative care. Mental health awareness and stress relief are important areas for our children to become skilled in. Again, the more we educate our children about the importance of issues pertaining to taking good care of themselves and model it ourselves, the easier it will be for them to succeed on this front.

Communication allows children to get along with others of all ages. It includes expressing themselves, listening to and understanding others. Communication is always vital, but especially when kids are in more challenging situations.

Community building allows children to feel a part of their families, classrooms, communities, and larger world. When kids feel connected to other people, they care about and respect them, the world, and their roles in it.

Responsibility naturally follows community, and children can then help solve problems as they learn more about their world. It takes courage and trust to be honest in their words and actions, living the lives they are capable of living. Children can take on these challenges when provided with responsibility, opportunities to solve problems, trust and honesty in their interactions with others, and courage to back them up.

It isn't always easy or fun being a parent or teacher in the moment, but the investment you make today will return to you in dividends. I am committed to helping you succeed in this journey, and I urge you to empower yourself so you can empower your kids. I hope you have been inspired by the children in this book and are motivated to add one or two items from it into your and your children's lives. Please contact me and tell me what you enjoyed or wished was included in this book. I'm happy to offer parents and teachers a thirty-minute complimentary coaching consultation to help you on your path. Please contact me at:

e-mail: Karen@KarenSzillat.com

website: www.EmpoweringTheChildren.com

I look forward to hearing from you!

With Gratitude,

— Karen Szillat

About the Author

★

Karen Szillat grew up in Princeton, Illinois in a family with six kids. She graduated from the University of Illinois and has twenty years experience in Early Childhood Education as a teacher, consultant, and administrator. She is happiest when interacting with groups of preschoolers in classroom settings. Karen was a recipient of the Washington State Exceptional Caregiver Award in 2010 for her work with young children.

Attending the Nuclear Age Peace Foundation's Peace Leadership Summer Workshop prompted Karen to add peace advocacy to her priorities. She is the author of the blog "Nurtured Children Grow" and on the Advisory Board for the Peaceful Educator Foundation. She has worked with hundreds of children in Illinois, Wisconsin, Germany, California, and Washington. She currently lives in Seattle with her husband, daughter, and piles of books.

About Szillat Coaching Services

★

I am happy to offer the following services:

- A thirty-minute complimentary coaching session to parents and teachers interested in empowering their children.

- On-going coaching services to parents and teachers by phone or on-site.

- Speaking engagements for parent and educational groups.

If you would like to contact me about parent coaching, teacher coaching, speaking engagements, to read my blog or provide comments and questions, please contact me at:

Karen@KarenSzillat.com

www.EmpoweringTheChildren.com